Quarterly Essay

AF583867

Quarterly Essay is published four times a year by Black Inc., an imprint of Schwartz Books Pty Ltd. Publisher: Morry Schwartz.

ISBN 9781760644994 ISSN 1444-884x

Subscriptions – 1 year print & digital (4 issues): $99.99 within Australia incl. GST. Outside Australia $134.99. 1 year digital only: $64.99.

Payment may be made by Mastercard or Visa, or by cheque made out to Schwartz Books. Payment includes postage and handling.

To subscribe, fill out and post the subscription card or form inside this issue, or subscribe online:

quarterlyessay.com
subscribe@quarterlyessay.com
Phone: 61 3 9486 0288

Correspondence should be addressed to:

The Editor, Quarterly Essay
22–24 Northumberland Street
Collingwood VIC 3066 Australia
Phone: 61 3 9486 0288 / Fax: 61 3 9011 6106
Email: quarterlyessay@blackincbooks.com

Editor: Chris Feik. Management: Elisabeth Young. Publicity: Anna Lensky. Design: Guy Mirabella. Associate Editor: Kirstie Innes-Will. Production Coordinator: Marilyn de Castro. Typesetting: Typography Studio.

Printed in Australia by McPherson's Printing Group. The paper used to produce this book comes from wood grown in sustainable forests.

LOSING IT

Can We Stop Violence Against Women and Children?

Jess Hill

It's 8.30 am in late November 2024, and in southwestern Sydney the heat is already overpowering. As I drive through the entrance to Campbelltown Hospital, the security guard gives me a nod and waves me towards a parking spot in the ambulance bay. As the engine dies, I sit for a few moments and steady myself. It's day three of the annual 16 Days of Activism against Gender-Based Violence, a high-energy time usually pumped with urgency and determination. But this year there's a distinctly different vibe: bone-deep exhaustion.

The killings have seemed relentless. By November, sixty-nine men have killed women they apparently once loved. Nine Aboriginal women have been killed in just five months in the Northern Territory. So full are the refuges that protect women and children from being murdered, and so scarce is the housing, that some refuge workers are now handing out tents. The need for help is escalating year on year, and the nature of sexual, domestic and family violence seems to be getting worse – according to many frontline workers, it's more complex and more severe. Globally, too, a brazen misogyny is on the march. In the country that bears the greatest influence over ours, a known sex offender has just been elected president on the coin of Silicon Valley "broligarchs," a victory celebrated by white supremacists on social media: "Your body, my choice. Forever."

I take a deep breath and walk to the hospital's lecture hall. Since my book *See What You Made Me Do* came out in 2019, I've decoded coercive control for audiences at almost 400 events across Australia. I'm an insider-outsider, and my professional and personal life is entwined with and enriched by thousands of others who work to end gendered violence. Today it's a full house, packed with frontline workers, doctors, police and advocates. I wave to friends and colleagues in the room and take a seat onstage. Next to me, a woman sits nervously, clutching her prepared notes. Her name is Theresa – a schoolteacher and mother of three, and one of a diverse group of victim-survivors helping the state government implement its new coercive control laws. Earlier this morning, she had told her story publicly for the first time – ten years to the day since she and her kids fled her sadistic ex-husband. "My eldest son Jack and I used to whisper the word 'prevention' to each other when we sensed his dad was about to go off," she tells me.

As we break for lunch, Theresa hands me a light-blue folder, meticulously organised with documents and photos: her evidence. "You'll also see in there a spreadsheet listing all the services that refused to help my kids," Theresa tells me, "because they are 'too complex.' I've got pages and pages of refusals."

Disclosures are common at events like this, though not usually so carefully prepared. But in every audience – whether they're locals at an Alice Springs community centre, maternal and child health nurses in Shepparton, or magistrates at a five-star hotel in Perth – there are always people waiting to share a story. Sometimes it's too much to say aloud, so they'll slip me a note and walk away. Other times we hold hands and let the tears come in silence. We just know.

As a nation, we *all* know so much more than we used to. Since 2014, when Rosie Batty first commanded Australia's attention after her son Luke was murdered by his father, the public voices of victim-survivors have increased in number and influence. Between the stories and the statistics, Australia has had a sharp and protracted awakening to the grim modern scale of men's violence against women and kids. Now, whenever the nation is convulsed by yet another homicide – especially when the victim is young, white and middle-class – newspaper front-pages cry "Enough!" and demand that governments *do something* to make it stop. The problem is: governments *are* doing something. They've committed record levels of funding to a national plan, they've changed laws, run summits and inquiries and taskforces – and yet the horror continues. In the statistics and in the bottomless supply of testimonies, like the one Theresa has just handed me.

On my way home, in the twenty minutes I have before collecting my daughter from school, I stop to grab a coffee and open Theresa's folder. As I start to read, I notice my breathing become shallow and tears sting my eyes. This folder documents coercive control at its most extreme. "Kill lists" of friends and family if Theresa ever tried to escape. Relentless degradation and humiliation. Isolation. Physical violence. Rape and sexual coercion. Weapons. Terrorising the kids physically and psychologically. In one plastic sleeve, a series of photos show two distressed little boys locked in a cage. Eight-year-old Jack growls at the camera. Theresa's ex-husband texted her those photos while she was at a parent–teacher night at her daughter's new school – as punishment for letting her daughter choose which school to attend. For his violence, her ex-husband had plenty of excuses. It was "appropriate punishment" to torture his kids, because he too had been hit as a child. It was Theresa's fault that he beat Jack with a bamboo stick – she was a teacher, and teachers had caned *him*. Page after page detailed the wreckage inflicted by a man so deformed by pain and rage he wanted friends and colleagues to call him Ivan, after the man he most admired: the serial killer Ivan Milat.

The documents also showed what Theresa and the kids faced when they miraculously escaped. Just to clear the first hurdle – getting him charged and convicted – required thousands of hours with police and lawyers, and interminable days in courthouse waiting rooms. Always the threat loomed, and the systems that should have helped them only made things worse.

In the shadow of child protection and family law proceedings, Theresa's three children self-harmed "at a level you could not comprehend," says Theresa, "trying to get control over the feelings, or relief from them." The two eldest also sought control over those feelings by becoming violent themselves. Like so many single mothers across Australia, Theresa had to set aside years of her life and every dollar she had to the mission of finding help for her kids, only to be told "over and over, 'Your children are too complex for our service.'" Her daughter Ruby self-harms to such a degree that she now requires iron and blood transfusions. Says Theresa: "I've basically been told to prepare to lose her."

At the back of Theresa's blue folder is a long letter from her then seventeen-year-old son, Jack. It was sent to the NSW State Parole Authority, protesting the planned release of his father, but the words were spoken directly to his dad: "WHY? This word plays in my head like a constant bell. I have asked Police, Lawyers, Doctors, Mental Health Professionals and Teachers, My Family and my Mum. No-one has an answer." In harrowing detail, Jack detailed how his dad's violence devastated his life.

> You used a staple gun on my legs. You turned my toy nerf guns and bullets into weapons to hurt me. You thought it was funny to shoot the bullets that had pins at the end of them. WHY?
>
> The way you spoke to me, always swearing and yelling at me, the threats, manipulation and emotional abuse were by far the worst. I still to this day fear the things you said to me will come true if you get parole. How will I protect my family and myself from you?
>
> I suffer from terrible nightmares. I wake up sweating and crying and go to my Mum for comfort and support. I still get flashbacks daily. There are thoughts in my head that are memories of the things that you did to me.
>
> For all my life, I needed your guidance as a Dad. You were meant to give me that support, the male role model of how to treat women and people in general. Instead all I saw and heard was how to manipulate, threaten, abuse, scare, bully and hurt people. Take what you wanted, use people then walk away from them.
>
> I just want to know one thing. WHY? WHY did you treat me

> like this? WHY did you destroy our family and hurt us. WHY? WHY? WHY?

It's Jack's pleading question to his father – to anyone who will listen – that is the heart of this essay. Why did Jack's father – an adopted boy who was beaten as a child – grow into a man who terrorised his wife and kids, ruining his own life in the process? What is it about his trajectory that is similar to – and different from – that of many men, from different cultures and backgrounds, who end up inflicting physical, sexual and psychological abuse on women and children? And how can we *interrupt* these violent trajectories, so this same old story doesn't play out over and again, one generation after the next?

Australian governments have promised to end gender-based violence – and no doubt they would sincerely like to see that happen. But while they have spent billions attending to this problem over the past decade, they are still only tinkering at the edges.

Things are not getting better. Our first National Plan to Reduce Violence Against Women and Their Children failed to achieve "a significant and sustained reduction in violence" by 2022. We could put this failure down to a lack of funding – and more money is certainly needed in many areas – but actually some of the best and most effective solutions cost *less* than what we are spending now.

This is a problem that goes deeper than funding. If we simply carry on doing more of what we've always done, there will *never* be enough money. As the outgoing social policy commissioner Natalie Siegel-Brown puts it, "By failing to address *why* people perpetrate, we are creating insatiable demand."

We see this insatiable demand in the statistics. Every year, the need for help escalates. In 2016, police across Australia were responding to an average of 5000 family violence incidents per week – a call-out every two minutes. That figure has now doubled to almost 10,000 reports per week – one every *minute*. In 2023, more than one in two police-recorded assaults were related to family and domestic violence (excluding Victoria), and since 2014 DV-related sexual assaults have increased by 78 per cent.

Nobody bears the brunt of this violence at the same rate or intensity as First

Nations women and children. Across Australia, most Aboriginal women are partnered with non-Indigenous men; the data tells us that Aboriginal women are thirty-two times more likely to be hospitalised and seven times more likely to be killed. That data, however, hasn't been updated in years – there's precious little contemporary data on what First Nations women and kids are experiencing. This is a huge roadblock for prevention because, as Djirra CEO Antoinette Braybrook says, "We can't change the things we don't measure." But we don't just leave this violence unmeasured – we leave it largely *unmentioned*. When Aboriginal women are murdered, they disappear out of sight and out of mind. As Chay Brown and Karla Glynn Braun wrote for the *Guardian*, three women being killed in Ballarat – population 115,000 – "quite rightly" inspired public outrage: "round-the-clock national media coverage, national marches and rallies … and a political and funding response." But when three Aboriginal women were killed around the same time in the Northern Territory town of Katherine – population 10,000 – there was "absolute damning silence."

By June 2025, First Nations women and children will finally have their own National Plan, designed by Aboriginal and Torres Strait Islander women and service providers. Winning government approval and funding for this new plan required unrelenting advocacy from countless leaders, including June Oscar, Muriel Bamblett and Professor Marcia Langton, experts like Hannah McGlade and Kyllie Cripps, and the two powerhouses behind Change the Record, Antoinette Braybrook and Cheryl Axleby-Keeffe. It's too early to say what exactly this standalone First Nations plan will look like, and what kind of targets it will set, but as Braybrook wrote in 2021, "it will not replicate the mistakes of the old [First] National Action Plan."

For non-Indigenous Australians, actions to prevent domestic, family and sexual violence at the national, state and territory level will be guided by the Second National Plan. This time, the plan's stated aim is not just to reduce violence but to end it – *within a single generation*.

No other country in the world has eradicated gendered violence. Australia is the only one that's even promised to do that. But for leaders and bureaucrats, there's a more fundamental challenge: do they have the courage to really try?

STICKING WITH THE PLAN

Australia had just emerged from almost a decade of Coalition government when the Second National Plan to End Violence Against Women and Their Children was released in October 2022. For feminists particularly, it was a kind of political whiplash: Scott Morrison, a man partial to religious visions, had suddenly been swept away on the hot wind of female anger, and in his place was Labor's Anthony Albanese, the son of a single mother who grew up in council housing. Australia now had a majority female government for the first time in Australian history, joined by six new female independents who had defeated Liberal members in previously safe seats.

The Second National Plan, drafted under the Morrison government, was released under a cloud. A furious open letter signed by forty-five prominent feminists, including Dr Anne Summers, Grace Tame, Khadija Gbla and Lucy Turnbull, slammed the draft plan as "largely a collection of statistics describing the issues, with noble sentiments and platitudes promising a future free from violence," but no clear vision for how that would be achieved. "We believe that a more robust analysis of how and why the first National Plan failed must be undertaken," it read. "Without this, the current draft Plan cannot claim to have 'learned' the lessons of the past decade, and so cannot hope to be more effective." My signature was also on this letter.

By the time of its release, the Second National Plan was different from the First in at least a few critical ways. While the majority of targets still aim for improvements to community attitudes, belief and knowledge, for the first time there were two clear targets for reducing violence: one to lower the rate of women killed by intimate partners by 25 per cent per year, and another to halve *all* forms of violence and abuse towards Aboriginal and Torres Strait Islander women and children by 2031. Children were, for the first time, recognised as "victim-survivors in their own right," rather than as mere extensions of their victim parent.

To achieve its goal of ending gender-based violence, the plan advises governments to stop violence before it starts. In its Performance Measurement

Plan, it's confident about how this will track: "prevalence of violence against women will remain static in the short and medium term, but will begin to decrease with improvements in gender equality and reductions in the drivers of violence."

What are the drivers? Gender inequality, disrespectful attitudes towards women, violence-condoning behaviour and rigid gender roles. But, the Second Plan cautions, improvements in these areas won't lead to an immediate reduction in violence. In fact, violence may, for some years, appear to *increase*. "Contrary to what we may see," it cautions, "it is important to recognise that an increase in rates does not necessarily mean gender-based violence is getting worse. It is more likely a reflection of peoples' growing awareness, understanding and confidence to come forward and seek formal support."

That logic – that an increase in reports is a *good* sign – has prevailed for at least the past decade. But for those who work at the coalface, it hasn't felt like a good sign for years. Frontline sexual assault workers say that it certainly *seems* like more women are being raped – and the data from their services shows that their clients are getting younger, and that the sexual violence used against them has become more severe. "Anal rape and strangulation especially are everyday experiences for women reporting to our service," says Di Macleod, who leads the Gold Coast Centre Against Sexual Violence. "Back in 1990, I can probably think of about four people who reported that."

But that's just anecdotal.

The sexual violence crime rate has risen every single year – reaching a 31-year high in 2023 – even as other crime categories have gone down.

We've been told to expect an increase in reports as more women seek help …

But what about the explosive Instagram poll by former private-school student Chanel Contos, which attracted thousands of graphic accounts of sexual violence, particularly from other private-school girls? Was this evidence that sexual violence was becoming worse – or at least different – for this generation?

Sexual violence has been a problem for millennia. Women of all ages have their stories.

Yes – but do older women have *this* many stories about being pressured to do anal, or being raped by a friend? Was it always routine for women to be choked during sex?

Wasn't *something* happening here?

For years, we had these clues – bits of data, testimonies, suspicions, signs. A lot of noise but no clear picture. Then out of that noise came national data.

The picture has clarified somewhat, and what it shows is shocking. Those frontline workers were right: more women *are* being raped. And it's not just the victims who are getting younger – it's their perpetrators. In 2024, the Australian Child Maltreatment Study (ACMS) showed that while child sexual abuse by *adult* perpetrators had decreased significantly, the rate of adolescent offending against other kids has – as reported by young Australians aged sixteen to twenty-four – *shot up*. The most common child sex offender now is another adolescent or child known to the victim.

What is the picture on sexual violence? At the same time as we've seen the sexual violence crime rate go up, the percentage of victim-survivors willing to report has gone *down*. Recent data from the Australian Bureau of Statistics shows that women are far less likely to report now than they were almost ten years ago. In 2016, 13 per cent of women reported their most recent incident of sexual assault by a male perpetrator to police. By 2021–22, that number plummeted to 8.3 per cent. And yet here we are in 2025, with the number of reported sexual assaults at a 31-year high. As sexual violence advocate Angela Lynch has consistently said, "We can no longer avoid the conclusion that this increase in reported sexual violence belies an increase in the amount of sexual violence that's being perpetrated." Sexual violence also has a newer form – image-based abuse – which is rising exponentially.

But most shocking of all was the statistic that fuelled angry public rallies nationwide: a 28 per cent rise in domestic homicides in 2022–23. Domestic homicide is the only murder category that has spiked, and we don't know why.

In other areas, the picture is changing – while physical violence is declining (in general, for both women *and* men), other coercive control methods are on the rise: between 2016 and 2021, the number of women who had their movements tracked by an ex-partner rose from 455,100 to 641,500. As we embark on the mission to end gender-based violence – apparently by around 2050 – we urgently need to consider two questions. After more than a decade of coordinated national effort on prevention, why are some forms of gender-based violence rising? And why is it getting *worse* for the very generation these efforts were supposed to benefit the most?

*

It wasn't supposed to turn out this way.

When the First National Plan was launched by the Gillard government in 2010, it was unprecedented – not just in Australia, but worldwide – for its strong focus on prevention. The commitment was ambitious: governments would seek to prevent violence by raising awareness, improving gender equality, bettering community attitudes towards violence, and teaching boys and girls how to think outside gender stereotypes and have more respectful relationships. This approach, combined with increased resourcing for the front line, was expected to reduce violence against women and their children by 2022. Minister for Women Kate Ellis said, "No government or group can tackle this problem alone – by working together and challenging the attitudes and behaviours that allow violence to occur, all Australian Governments are saying a very loud 'no' to violence."

The theory of change underpinning the First Plan was complex: gendered drivers set the necessary context in which violence against women and children could thrive, so if we tackled *them*, this kind of violence would become less common. Other priorities, like supporting victim-survivors and holding perpetrators accountable, were of course vitally important. But gender equality was the key to solving men's violence against women and their children.

This fast became gospel. In 2014, when *Guardian Australia* asked Australia's state and territory police commissioners to diagnose the cause of domestic violence, they overwhelmingly named society's attitudes towards women. "We are all responsible for shifting social norms that blame, excuse, minimise and justify violence against women and their children," wrote the

Tasmanian commissioner, Darren Hine. "Addressing this issue is going to require lasting generational change. Lead by example. Challenge others. Own the change."

The optimism was infectious, and there were high hopes: Australia was going to be a world leader in prevention. The plan set out a confident timeline for the expected pace of change: by 2019, physical and sexual violence would be declining, and fewer children would be growing up with domestic violence. It got off to a strong start. The first phase established several national institutions: the family violence helpline 1800 RESPECT, the Australian National Research Organisation for Women's Safety (ANROWS), and Our Watch, a national agency to direct gender-based violence-prevention efforts across Australia.

In 2013, just as the First National Plan was entering its second phase, the Labor government was ousted and Tony Abbott – the self-described "political lovechild" of John Howard and Bronwyn Bishop – handed it to his new minister for social services, Kevin Andrews. Over the next six years, the plan would be passed like a hot potato from Andrews to Scott Morrison, then to Christian Porter, Dan Tehan, Paul Fletcher and, finally, Anne Ruston, who was the social services minister when it came time to announce the National Plan's fourth stage – "Turning the Corner" – in August 2019.

But no corner had been turned. In August 2019, Commonwealth, state and territory leaders flew the white flag: there would be no substantial reduction in violence against women and their children by 2022. In fact, the statistics would remain static for the short to medium term – ten years at least – but *would* steadily begin to drop as community attitudes towards violence improved, rigid gender norms loosened, women gained greater independence and more young people were taught how to have respectful relationships. This forecast, which kicked violence reduction into the long grass, was based on modelling provided to governments by Our Watch.

It was a tacit admission of failure from governments, gussied up with reassurance: Australia was still on the right path, gender-based violence *was* preventable and, with the right investment and focus, the statistics *would* start to improve. To get there, the Morrison government announced it would double down on prevention and make it a key priority: "We want to change attitudes to violence and help those who think violence is an option to stop," said Prime Minister Scott Morrison, announcing $20.9 million for Our Watch to set up a "national prevention hub."

The plan may have been failing, but governments were staying the course. The theory of change was sound – it just needed more time.

*

Reader, I'm afraid this is where we must put on our policy gumboots and wade through the mangroves of Australia's prevention strategy. To really get our heads around the business of violence prevention, we need to become familiar with the 2015 strategy document that guides it, *Change the Story: A shared framework for the primary prevention of violence against women and their children in Australia*.

Developed by Our Watch, with support from the Victorian Health Promotion Foundation and ANROWS, *Change the Story* was hailed as a world first. Although other violence-prevention frameworks existed, no other country had ever developed its own framework. *Change the Story* had the key to a problem that had dogged humans for millennia – the secret formula for creating a country where "women live free from violence." Writing in *The Conversation*, RMIT's Anastasia Powell, a technical adviser to the framework, and Our Watch's Dr Emma Partridge and Dr Lara Fergus were exuberant: "Violence against women is not inevitable. Rather, it is driven by a series of complex and entrenched but changeable social and environmental factors. In other words, violence against women is preventable. We can change this story. A new framework shows how."

It was released to the public with huge fanfare in November 2015. "This is a watershed moment," enthused Our Watch chair Natasha Stott Despoja. "With *Change the Story*, we are better placed than ever before to end violence against women and children in Australia." Standing alongside the former Democrats senator were the Coalition ministers stewarding the National

Plan: Minister for Women Michaelia Cash and Minister for Social Services Christian Porter. Cash was typically vigorous: "To change the story that ends in violence, we must begin with gender equality and respect … Reducing violence against women and their children is a national priority and I want 2015 to be the turning point in our response."

It was a remarkable turnaround for Australian feminists. Just two short months earlier, Australia had been ruled by a paternalistic Catholic who'd appointed himself Minister for Women. Then, within a matter of hours, Abbott had been vanquished and a new prime minister was in charge. Like a silver-haired Glinda the Good, Malcolm Turnbull landed suddenly and announced a new era for Oz: women and girls would be respected as equals, and fighting gender-based violence would be a national priority. Immediately he announced $100 million in extra funding and made his now famous declaration: "Disrespecting women does not always result in violence against women. But all violence against women begins with disrespecting women."

It felt like a new era had dawned. "The elephant in the room is no longer being ignored," wrote Our Watch's then CEO, Mary Barry, "The research is consistent and the message is now loud and clear – we cannot stop Australia's scourge of violence against women without squarely tackling gender inequality." Australia had already led the world with innovative efforts to fight smoking and HIV. Now was its chance to set a new world standard for violence prevention. This would require courage, innovation, collaboration and a dose of good faith. "We have nothing we can look at in another country and say, 'Look at how well it worked over there,'" Dr Lara Fergus told *Guardian Australia* in 2016. "We are asking for leadership."

Change the Story was not just a world first, it was also markedly different to other best-practice prevention frameworks like those used by the World Health Organization and the Prevention Collaborative. Such frameworks listed multiple intersecting risk factors such as childhood maltreatment, substance abuse, a weak criminal justice system and a culture of parental dominance over children (to name a few), *alongside* gendered risk factors, like harmful attitudes and gender inequality. *Change the Story* did something new and different: it arranged risk factors into a hierarchy, positioning four "gendered drivers" above the "reinforcing factors." These four gendered drivers were: the condoning of violence against women; men's control of decision-making and limits to women's independence in public and private life; rigid gender roles and stereotyped constructions of masculinity and femininity; and male peer relations that emphasise aggression and disrespect towards women.

The gendered drivers were the most important to target, because these set the social conditions that consistently predict, or "drive," higher levels of violence against women. Reinforcing factors – though they did make violence more likely – were not sufficient on their own to cause it. The reinforcing factors were: condoning of violence in general; experience of and exposure to violence; factors that weaken pro-social behaviour, such as stress, environmental factors, disasters and crises, male-dominated settings and heavy alcohol consumption; and resistance and backlash to prevention and gender equality efforts.

Explaining why *Change the Story* took this different approach, Fergus explained that, thanks to "an explosion of research in the past decade … the old approach that there was a 'shopping list' of factors causing violence against women has become more sophisticated – factors such as alcohol or mental illness or the experience of violence in the perpetrator's childhood filter through the key issue of gender inequality."

The solution was clear: if you direct most of your effort to addressing the gendered drivers, the reinforcing factors will be less of a problem, because they don't cause violence on their own. It's kind of like trickle-down economics, only for violence.

This new focus was explained in the video Our Watch released to go with *Change the Story*. As Gay Alcorn described it for *Guardian Australia*:

> "This is a story about a boy and a girl," it begins. The girl is told "how pretty she is, never how clever she is, that if she wears a short dress, she's asking for it." As for the boy, "he learned that women aren't equal to men from a very early age." This is a story of "how gender inequality contributes to the murder of around one Australian

woman almost every week." The video raises no other factor involved in domestic violence.

Change the Story explicitly advised governments to elevate "primary prevention" – which targets the whole population – above and beyond other forms of prevention that work with at-risk groups.

To explain why, Our Watch uses a metaphor called the "river of prevention." Imagine you're looking at a river. Upstream, there are people standing on dry land; these are the people who haven't experienced violence – the target audience for primary prevention. Downstream, there are hands in the river waving for help – that's where we throw in the "early intervention" life rafts (also known as "secondary prevention"), for those most at risk of experiencing or perpetrating violence. Further downstream, people are already drowning. That's where we see the ambulance parked for crisis response (or tertiary prevention) – to help those who've been harmed to recover, and thus to help prevent future violence. The moral of this story is that if governments want more Australians to stay safe and dry, they should direct the lion's share of prevention funding to primary prevention.

The vision in *Change the Story* sounded exciting and incredibly ambitious: to work with "all people, across all levels of society, to change and transform the social context in which violence against women is able to flourish." It proposed to do this in a variety of ways: including media campaigns to counter harmful stereotypes, and respectful relationships education at schools to reach young people while their attitudes were still malleable.

But not everybody was so hopeful. In 2016, Michael Thorn, then CEO of the Foundation for Alcohol Research and Education, wrote to Turnbull expressing his disappointment that the role of alcohol was being "neglected in the ongoing family violence narrative." There were low-cost interventions that could achieve "immediate reductions in domestic violence," and the refusal to act on these "could sustain and increase the suffering of women and children." Although *Change the Story* noted alcohol, he said, it did not recommend any regulatory action to address it. "This heavy emphasis on gender inequality is excluding recourse to policy change that will reduce risk and prevent violence," he wrote, adding: "I imagine those concerned about other contributing factors, such as mental health, social exclusion, and economic disadvantage, are similarly pessimistic."

As Thorn's letter indicated, not everybody was enthusiastic about *Change the Story*. In fact, there was still significant disagreement over exactly what caused gender-based violence and how best to address it. That tension was especially palpable throughout Victoria's landmark Royal Commission into Family Violence in 2015. As Commissioner Marcia Neave later described:

> It was put strongly to the Royal Commission that family violence is largely, if not entirely attributable to gender inequality, and that the most effective strategy for reducing violence is to improve the situation of women in areas such as the workforce and public life. Other commentators argued that gender inequality does not necessarily account for violence by men and women against children, by adult children against older parents, or for violence against people with disabilities or within same sex relationships. It was also argued that improving gender equality would not address other factors which contribute to family violence or affect individual abusers, including social disadvantage and unemployment, mental illness, economic inequality, and drug and alcohol abuse.

Neave was relieved that the commission did not have to formally identify the accepted cause of family violence. "In my view this would be a fruitless task, because complex social phenomena like family violence usually involve an interaction between many factors."

By 2019, however, governments considered that dispute settled. Australia was united behind *Change the Story*. Gender-based violence would be reduced once there were significant improvements to gender equality, social norms and community attitudes.

For the Morrison government, a focus on norms and attitudes was evidently very appealing. In the 2022 election campaign, it pledged an extra $189 million for family, domestic and sexual violence, including

$104 million for Our Watch (a 65 per cent funding increase), $47.8 million on a campaign encouraging men to hold each other accountable, and $32 million on a campaign to help parents talk to their children about consent and respectful relationships, a follow-up to the government's now infamous milkshake video.

There was a lot of confidence about the potential for societal change outlined in *Change the Story*, but a surprising lack of detail about what it would take to achieve it. In its modelling, Our Watch predicted that violence rates would remain static until primary prevention was properly resourced and the gendered drivers substantially improved: "then – and only then – will we start to see a decrease in rates of violence against women." Once prevention was properly resourced, and with the necessary leadership from government and civil society, there would also be a decline in the strength of the reinforcing factors. There was, however, a distinct lack of detail on what it would take to reduce such entrenched social problems as harmful alcohol use and socioeconomic inequality. And on what basis was it decided that, once the gendered drivers (and reinforcing factors) improved, violence would then be expected to fall within six to ten years? If this strategy hasn't been tried anywhere else in the world, what was the benchmark for this assertion? As Dr Emma Partridge had told *Guardian Australia* in 2016, "Of course it's a hypothesis, because no one's ever tried to change the gender norms, structures and practices in a society at a population level before." What exactly had changed to calcify this "hypothesis" into "fact"?

*

There is no doubt that gender inequality is both a cause and a consequence of men's violence against women and children. There's also no doubting the sincerity and determination of those trying to address this. In 2019, when Australians learned that the rates of violence would *not* decline as promised, Our Watch CEO Patty Kinnersly urged people to keep the faith. "We do know that people can unlearn their attitudes, and we know that violence against women is preventable. We have to stick with it," she told *The Project*.

"The evidence tells us we have to address the underlying drivers of violence against women. We have to promote, normalise and celebrate gender equality in all the places we spend our time … and each of us has to understand what our sphere of influence is." Children developed their attitudes in line with what they saw in various "settings" – at schools, at sport, in workplaces and on television – and "if they're not getting great role-modelling in one part of their life, we want them to be saturated by good examples of healthy, respectful relationships in other parts of their life." In the face of otherwise demoralising statistics, this was an empowering vision – a Rosie the Riveter call-out to Australians to roll up their sleeves and join the mission to end gender-based violence. *We Can Do It!*

It also evoked nostalgia for a simpler time – when people's values and attitudes were shaped by a mainstream culture, and by the family, friends and peers in their local orbit. But by 2019 the halcyon days of a homogenised media and predominantly local life were over, and the old methods of cultural persuasion were being fast superseded. Increasingly, Australians were spending time in a setting that was virtually lawless, and where government-funded messaging had very little traction. For almost fifteen years, social media and smartphones had globalised everybody's "sphere of influence" – yet there was virtually no comprehension of this in the fourth phase of the First National Plan.

While Australia was singularly focused on physical points of contact, the real battle for young hearts and minds was being waged online. And for young men seeking empowerment, life advice or perhaps a community of other gamers to chat to while they played *Fortnite* and *Minecraft*, there was a growing subculture waiting to meet them. The "manosphere" was still a relatively new term in 2019. But feminists had been raising the alarm for years, warning about a disparate network of misogynistic subcultures, including pick-up artists, incels and MGTOWs ("men going their own way"). By 2019, these groups – and a cast of imitators and copycats – were increasingly shaping the views of some young men. Only now a whole new army of male influencers was selling self-improvement and male empowerment, along with an increasingly persuasive message: feminism is a conspiracy, it defies the laws of nature, it is undermining your rights and opportunities, and it must be opposed.

In a 2023 survey of more than 1300 boys by The Man Cave, one in four Australian boys of secondary school age said they looked up to Andrew Tate as a role model, attracted to what they described as his "inspirational work ethic; his relatable opinions; his confidence and bravery to fight for 'what he feels is right'; and his willingness to defend men and traditional male values." Meanwhile, young women have moved into their own progressive echo chambers and feel increasingly alienated from young men.

As the social scientist Dr Alice Evans writes, this transition to ubiquitous online connectivity has seen us all "forging tribes with ideological allies across the world, while paradoxically spending more time in solitude." This shows up in dating statistics – more young people are single today than any point in modern history. "Solitude and the rise of singles mean fewer opportunities for cross-gender empathy and understanding," writes Evans, "Men and women increasingly inhabit separate social worlds. We increasingly become *economic competitors*." Which only makes the sexist narratives of "manfluencers" more persuasive: if it weren't for feminism, women would need a male partner for economic security. Now they don't need you – and they're taking your jobs away. Opposition leader Peter Dutton has leaned into this explicitly, warning in early 2025 that young men were "fed up" with being overlooked for jobs simply because of workplace gender quotas.

Fighting for a return to traditional gender norms is now framed as "the new punk" – a pushback against a mainstream culture that embraces progressivism as its "religion." There is a noxious slipstream from misogyny to white supremacy and race-baiting: as Aboriginal and Torres Strait Islander author Thomas Mayo wrote in *The Saturday Paper*, even his "progressive algorithm" can't keep out content about "lazy, unfaithful or conniving women" and "male victimhood," as well as "a massive volume of footage of people of colour drinking, fighting, committing crimes or being disrespectful." Whereas Mayo's generation "was influenced by the adults we looked up to – who threw around racist or sexist tropes, often unwittingly – today we are all being fed such ignorant views through our phones."

In late 2024, ASIO chief Mike Burgess pegged an alarming increase in youth radicalisation to the influence of social media: "Now, individuals can be self-radicalised, and the process can take days and weeks rather than months and years … If a user spends just 10 minutes looking at incel material, the algorithm starts recommending more and more violent misogynist propaganda, including posts glorifying incel terrorists," he said. "In one generation, we have allowed our children full access to alleyways, content and people that they would not be able to access in the physical world."

Incels occupy the extreme end of the spectrum, but there is growing evidence that a broader backlash is darkening the attitudes of a significant minority of young men. In 2024, 20 per cent of Australian men aged eighteen to twenty-nine agreed that, "if necessary, feminism should be violently resisted," and over 12 per cent of all male respondents agreed that women's sexual autonomy should be denied.

Sector leaders have told me that the online environment caught them by surprise. *The data is scary on young men*, they say, *and we are behind*.

THE BACKLASH FACTORY

The online environment is the influence factory for backlash, but while we spend a lot of time angsting over high-profile influencers like Andrew Tate, they're really just the guys on the factory floor. In the meantime, we've paid very little attention to who's running the business: a broad coalition of political leaders and "anti-rights" groups that are well organised, well financed and extremely effective.

In her travels to fifty-five countries over the past eighteen months, Australia's gender equality ambassador, Stephanie Copus Campbell, has seen the incredible force of this backlash in almost every corner of the world. When we first met – in surreal circumstances, on our way to a round-table meeting with Queen Camilla – Campbell had just returned from overseas, and the backlash was at the front of her mind. "I'm usually an optimistic person, but I'm not feeling optimistic about this," she said. What Campbell told me during our few minutes together gave me an inkling of just how coordinated this backlash was, and the scale of it. It's virtually impossible for a senior public servant to get approval to talk publicly about something this politically hot, especially in this climate, so I went digging myself. The picture that emerged was of a hydra-headed monster spitting venom at multiple points of influence – from disaffected young men sitting alone in their bedrooms to diplomats hammering out multilateral negotiations at the United Nations.

At the highest level, the backlash targets multilateral negotiations. Russia – now joined by the United States – is leading an intensifying pushback against rights, arguing (successfully) for the removal of terms such as "gender" and "bodily autonomy" from international agreements. This is all about targeting the international rules-based order. Putin doesn't need weaponry to destabilise the West – he does that by systematically undermining multilateral negotiations on everything from food security to trade and humanitarian relief, by weakening legal frameworks and eroding the power and influence of international institutions. To support its agenda,

Russia also exports disinformation – spreading conspiracy theories, targeting women and LGBTIQA+ people, and positioning progressive policies as proof of a decadent West in decline.

The next level down is the broader anti-rights agenda that's being driven by international groups – non-government organisations, foundations, Russian oligarchs and right-wing Christian groups based in Europe, America and Russia. They're coordinated, strategic and incredibly well funded. We see their footprints everywhere: the overturning of *Roe v. Wade*, anti-abortion laws in Poland and anti-LGBTIQA+ legislation in Uganda. They're funding political candidates, scholarships and university curriculums. They're funding bot factories and disinformation. They're funding think-tanks like the Heritage Foundation and Project 2025 (described recently by US Republican senator Angus King as "nothing less than a blueprint for the shredding of the Constitution and the transition of our country to authoritarian rule").

These groups can outspend progressive movements. From 2009 to 2018, more than fifty anti-gender groups spent US$707.2 million ($1.14 billion) influencing political agendas around the world, lobbying and manoeuvring to reverse gains in the areas of gender, racial and same-sex equality. They have a long list of targets: same-sex marriage, comprehensive sexuality education, laws and protections against gender-based violence, contraception and even divorce. They also block action on climate change and fund anti-vaccination campaigns (which was particularly devastating during COVID). In developing countries particularly, they are weaponising decolonisation narratives to turn populations against so-called "Western" values.

Mainstream support for this agenda is then mobilised through various media – podcasts, social media, forums, the dark web – with the help of high-profile influencers (including Andrew Tate) and an army of copycats who exploit the growing social isolation of some young men to pull them into the misogynistic space and use them as foot soldiers. The social isolation of some young men is becoming dangerous: in one recent American study, two out of three men aged eighteen to twenty-three felt like nobody really knew them; around a third hadn't spent time with anyone outside their house in the past week; 44 per cent said they'd had suicidal thoughts in the past fortnight; almost half said their online lives were more satisfying than their offline lives; around a third said they couldn't find an intimate partner; more than half agreed that men now have it harder than women; and 60 per cent were regularly watching porn. "In short," the report concluded, "boys and men are not all right, and their discomfort and confusion are associated with their eroding support for gender and racial equity."

The last level is tech-facilitated gender-based violence, which disproportionately targets women, girls, human rights workers and LGBTIQA+ advocates, with the explicit intent of pushing them out of public space. Ambassador Campbell has herself been targeted, as has Australia's e-safety commissioner, Julie Inman-Grant, most aggressively by Elon Musk after the e-Safety Commission took X/Twitter to court to enforce a take-down notice for graphic videos of the Wakeley church stabbing in Western Sydney. "He issued a dog whistle to 181 million users around the globe," Inman-Grant told the ABC, and she was flooded with death threats and abuse, while her family members, including her three kids, were doxxed. It was so serious that Inman-Grant had to restrict her public appearances and engage the Australian Federal Police.

Broadcasting prevention messages into this febrile and dangerous atmosphere is not just difficult but fraught with risk. These backlash actors take the language of pro-rights activists – terms like "toxic masculinity" – and use it against them. To their audience, they say, "See, we told you. *They* hate young men. *They're* trying to push their Western values. *They* want to take over the world." Across the world, the belief that gender equality policies harm boys and men is fast gaining traction.

And that's not just coming from boys and men. According to the most recent iteration of Plan International Australia's Gender Compass, an online survey of more than 2000 Australians aged over sixteen, that view was also held by a significant minority of women. Based on a further ten focus groups split by gender, the report found that many of these women "were very concerned about men being demonised and were uncomfortable with the 'negativity' propagated by 'staunch feminists' and the 'activist class' whom they see as trying to pit men and women against each other." Gender Compass split respondents into six segments according to their views on gender equality: "Trailblazer" (19 per cent), "Hopeful" (24 per cent), "Conflicted" (12 per cent), "Moderate" (23 per cent), "Indifferent" (6 per cent) and "Rejector" (17 per cent). Women in the Moderate, Rejector and Conflicted segments held these strong concerns, typified by this comment from a 57-year-old woman from Western Australia: "Men are reviled by society at the moment. They're considered to be toxic no matter what they do … I feel particularly sorry for young men and boys because they've been raised where they're basically treated like they're guilty, just by the fact that they're a man."

Trailblazer men were happy to talk openly about the harms of patriarchy, like this 47-year-old from regional New South Wales: "We have a responsibility to examine the ways we've benefited from the privilege and then think 'Are there ways that we're actually perpetuating the patriarchy that we might not be aware of?' And what can we do to make society better and more equal and safer?" But among others, particularly in the "Conflicted" segment, there was pronounced discomfort at traditional gender roles being undermined. There was also fear, notably among "Moderate" men, that they may unintentionally say something offensive or be perceived as a "creep"; this was leading them to withdraw from engaging with women in social and work settings. Rejector men were more staunch: they believed men were being discriminated against, and unfairly blamed for the actions of the minority.

Most respondents agreed that gender equality was important – but there was a lot of confusion over that term. "Rejectors," for example, dismissed women's experiences as being due to personal choices, biological differences or the actions of a few bad men. Others were more ambiguous: said one 27-year-old "Moderate" man: "I can relate to [the phrase] equal opportunity … and I agree with *fair treatment* pretty strongly. In terms of *rights for women and girls*, not really. I understand what it's trying to say, but I don't think that's a strong message, because everyone should have rights." Almost 60 per cent of respondents believed that, in Australia, gender equality was close to being achieved, or already had been. For them, the movement to promote rights and opportunities for women and girls seemed out of proportion. They were also more likely to believe that such initiatives will penalise men and boys and put barriers in their way.

As Plan International CEO Susanne Legena explained, Gender Compass revealed "the sheer amount of confusion, ambivalence and disagreement there is in Australian society about what exactly constitutes gender equality (or inequality) … Nearly the same proportion of Australians believe equality for women has gone too far as believe that [in]equality between genders is a dire issue [to be addressed]. And then there's a big group in the middle, many of whom we're not really talking to very effectively, who have mixed feelings and mixed attitudes around this issue."

What Gender Compass did find was "an appetite for gender equality solutions that address concerns about the challenges women *and* men are facing." Australia's gender equality ambassador echoes this when she talks about her working definition of the term: that every person has every opportunity to meet their full potential, regardless of their gender. More often than not, the barriers to equality are highest for women and girls, but that's not always the case. In education, for example, nearly half of Australian boys are falling behind the national literacy benchmark by Year 9, while Australia has the world's worst gender gap in maths and science achievement for girls. Gender equality doesn't have to be a zero-sum game.

*

By mid-2024, a woman was being killed every four days. In April, after five women and one man were stabbed to death at Bondi Junction's Westfield shopping centre, public anger and grief hit boiling point and tens of thousands of Australians poured onto the streets in cities and towns across the country, demanding that governments "do something" to stop men murdering women.

By then, as this essay will discuss, Australia was having a long-overdue, albeit difficult, conversation about our violence-prevention strategy. For the first time, journalists were starting to question whether our current prevention strategy was ever going to show results. "Intimate-partner homicides are on the rise, despite record levels of investment in prevention," observed *The Project*'s Waleed Aly. Some frontline leaders, too, were broadcasting their scepticism: "We can't just wait for some time, thirty years in the future, where we *might* solve it by having conversations about respect," said Annabelle Daniel, chair of the peak body for domestic violence services, DVNSW, and CEO of Women's Community Shelters. "There are concrete interventions that we need to make now. The big elephants in the room are things like alcohol, gambling and the unrestricted access young men and boys have to hardcore pornography."

Our Watch was under fire for being too disconnected from the front line, and *Change the Story* was being criticised for marginalising the role of critical risk factors like alcohol and poverty. On this, longtime journalist, researcher and educator on gender-based violence Jane Gilmore was scathing: "Preventing gender-based violence requires more than rigid adherence to a flawed document and almost all national prevention funding going to a single organisation with no frontline presence."

Into this debate, Our Watch released a short report card, "Tracking Progress in Prevention." While its last monitoring report in 2020 ran to 350 pages, this update was only fourteen pages and seemed to have been hastily prepared. But there was good news to share: as Our Watch explained, prevention was "showing encouraging signs of progress and heading in the right direction – and we need to stay the course." Across its key data points – from attitudes to prevalence rates – every area was either making "good progress" or remaining "stable." One area of "good progress" was the overwhelming support Australians show for gender equality. Under the headline "Most Australians know gender inequality and violence against women are significant issues" it said, "90 per cent of Australians agree that gender equality is important," and cited Gender Compass.

When I first read that, I did a double take and checked to see if the report card provided any further context. It didn't. Nowhere did it mention that

Gender Compass had also found that almost 60 per cent of Australians thought gender equality had mostly or already been achieved, that a significant minority believed that men were experiencing discrimination, and that 17 per cent self-identified as outright "Rejectors" of the movement for women's rights. It's hard to fathom that a national agency would so wilfully misrepresent a statistic like this – especially one so central to its agenda.

The Second Plan also has an upbeat appraisal of Australian attitudes to gender equality: "Since the 2010–2022 National Plan," it reads, "fewer Australians hold attitudes that support violence against women, and most Australians support gender equality." The plan is not misrepresenting statistics, but it *is* using old data from 2017. Given the "sheer amount of ambivalence, confusion and disagreement" there is about the term, it's worth reminding ourselves how the plan defines gender *inequality*: "A social condition ... [which is] the direct result of patriarchal systems that privilege the needs, interests and behaviours of men over women, and that permeate many aspects of Australian society and institutions." Does the government believe that distinctly feminist definition of gender inequality resonates with "most" Australians?

I'm not trying to land some cheap gotcha moment. But this misperception of Australians' attitudes is emblematic of a big problem: a fundamental disconnect between the assumptions that drive prevention work, and the values and beliefs of the people it's trying to reach. If prevention agencies presume every Australian is or wants to be, in Gender Compass terms, a "Trailblazer," taxpayers will waste millions more on messaging that doesn't just preach to the converted, but further alienates the exact people it most needs to influence. Similarly, if Our Watch refuses to acknowledge what is right in front of people's eyes – in this case, that some of the violence *is* getting worse and attitudes towards gender equality are becoming more polarised and hostile – even the converted may stop listening to them.

We're living in dangerous times. The conditions for violence-prevention work – and feminism in general – are hostile and getting worse. As I write, Donald Trump has just been inaugurated as the forty-seventh President of the United States. Several of the authors behind Project 2025 are now key figures in his administration. Seated directly behind Trump at his inauguration ceremony were America's tech titans – Elon Musk, Mark Zuckerberg, Jeff Bezos and the CEOs of Apple and Google. This is a massive inflection point for global culture. As Damon Beres wrote for *The Atlantic*, these men "control the tools that billions of people around the world use to communicate, to receive information, to be entertained, to navigate and understand the world."

Simon Welsh, from Redbridge political consultancy, says the new political force in Australia mirrors the energy among American voters in 2024: "The sense of disempowerment and alienation among young men means that what they want is a 'shock' to a system that they no longer believe operates in their interests." It might have been fed-up women who helped bring Prime Minister Albanese to power in 2022, but now Labor is being warned that its major problem is "very grumpy" men.

In no way am I advising a surrender to these prevailing conditions. But prevention agencies – and governments – must be ready and able to adapt to them.

The stakes could not be higher – which is why we need to have an open and honest debate about what's working and what isn't. As Annabelle Daniel told *The Saturday Paper*, "This literally has as the endpoint the lives of women and children. It is a critical conversation that we have to have. And what we can't let get in the way is organisational ego, research ego, or organisational self-perpetuation, or more funding, or any of those things. Our eye has to be on solving the problem."

In November 2024, a few days before Theresa handed me her blue evidence folder, social services minister Amanda Rishworth sat down for a podcast interview with *Guardian Australia's* political editor, Karen Middleton. With the 16 Days of Activism about to begin, Middleton asked Rishworth, "Are these occasions really just another reminder of how intractable and enormous this problem is?"

"I've spoken a lot about how we need consistent and persistent effort," Rishworth replied. "If we think about some of the drivers of gender-based violence, they are going to take some time to turn around; it's attitudes towards women, it's attitudes towards accepting misogyny."

But those attitudes seemed to be going in the wrong direction, Middleton countered, and popular influencers are openly championing the hatred of women. The government had just launched a new stage of the "Stop It at the Start" campaign, she noted, but that just raised another question: "How do you have an effect with just an ad campaign up against such a powerful force?"

Rishworth conceded that "it's a really challenging environment to work in." There was no "silver bullet," she said, "but we've got to be working with young men; they've got to be part of the conversation, and we've got to broaden our understanding out there in the community about what gender-based violence is." Since 2016, the government has invested $115 million in Stop It at the Start, which aims to "reset" the attitudes of young people through motivating the adults in their lives to reflect on their own misplaced attitudes and have better conversations about gender equality and respect.

Dr Rebecca Huntley is one of Australia's leading experts on social trends. She spends an inordinate amount of time in focus groups, listening to regular Australians answer questions about pressing social issues such as climate change and gender equality, most recently for two ongoing surveys: Climate Compass and Gender Compass. It's been her life's work to observe how Australians feel, think and act – and to figure out what it takes to change their minds. Even when the conditions are right, she says, attitudes are incredibly hard to shift. "Global studies show that for every climate-driven extreme weather event, the best possible outcome is a 1 per cent increase in people who are concerned about climate. After the Black Summer fires and the extreme floods, we had a 2 per cent increase in the percentage of people who are alarmed, and that was really just an acceleration for the group of people who were already concerned. Millions of animals have to die, billions of dollars in property destroyed – you have to see the smoke from space – and you *might* get a 1 per cent shift in people's attitudes. That's how hard it is."

It's not just that changing attitudes is difficult, she says – it's that such changes don't always stick, and hard-fought gains can be washed away from one generation to the next. "After years of looking at how people behave, I've abandoned the idea that we're on some kind of smooth trajectory towards improvement. We have action and reaction, and cycles."

In Huntley's extensive experience, changing attitudes to gender is even *harder* than changing attitudes on climate. Right now, as Gender Compass clearly shows, "we are seeing sentiment stagnating and polarising on gender equality, with Australians believing we've solved the issue … If the measure of success is in shifting attitudes, we've set ourselves up to fail, and we're putting an enormous amount of energy into something that is very difficult to do in a short period of time." For Australia, the deadline is close: "a single generation" takes us to 2050, at the latest. Huntley believes that campaigners should keep "chipping away" at shifting attitudes, but they should do so with clear eyes. "I think we have to remain intellectually curious about what's actually happening, and occasionally step back and go, *That's not working*, and reach for new tools."

The Australian government measures changes to community attitudes through the National Community Attitudes Survey, which has been running since 2009. Over the phone, interviewers gauge opinions, beliefs and knowledge on a vast range of issues related to gender-based violence and gender equality. The results reflect Huntley's concerns. While the NCAS showed a steady improvement over time in attitudes that reject violence against women – from 63 per cent in 2009 to 68 per cent in 2021 – it showed no significant change in attitudes towards domestic violence between 2017 and 2021. That's especially troubling because in modern Australian history there's never been a greater period of heightened awareness and advocacy for domestic violence. If we couldn't achieve a significant change in attitudes over that period, what would it take?

The NCAS results demonstrate something else: that an overall change in *attitudes* for a certain group may not correlate with a change in *behaviour*. We see this disconnect showing up not just across large survey samples but in individuals. Psychologists call it *attitude–behaviour inconsistency*: when a person's actions don't match their stated feelings or beliefs.

The NCAS Youth Report, which surveyed 1700 Australians aged sixteen to twenty-four years, showed that between 2017 and 2021 there was a significant increase in the number of young people who rejected attitudes that objectify women and disregard consent. And yet, over recent years, the rate of adolescents sexually assaulting other children also increased. So what makes us so confident that an improvement in community attitudes will foreshadow a decline in violence?

"I measure attitudes knowing how contradictory people can be," says Huntley. "That shows up particularly in the realm of violence and control. Because [the tendency to be abusive] is something deeper than culture. It's deep within the body; a psychological impulse."

Huntley knows the story of gendered violence in her bones. "I'm someone who's grown up with a lot of rage inside me. My parents put that inside me," she tells me. As a child, her father subjected her to intense physical violence and emotional abuse – a harrowing experience she documents in her recent memoir, *Sassafras*. "I'm completely in awe of people whose parents physically beat them up as children [and] who *don't* do that. How amazing, not to carry that through." Huntley says her father was the poster boy for attitude–behaviour inconsistency. "My father was a professor of law: he was a champion of women in the workplace and, you know, supported so many women to become judges," she says. "If you had given him a survey, he would have ticked all the right boxes. And yet he was just a horrible father."

In the field of mental health, the gap between our stated (explicit) beliefs and our deeply held (implicit) beliefs has long been understood. On a subject as deeply personal as violence, it is very difficult to ascertain how a person will behave when, for example, they are drunk, or when their attachment issues are triggered, if all you're doing is simply asking them a set of questions in a controlled environment.

Survey results can also be distorted by something quite purposeful – social desirability bias. In other words, when some people answer a survey over the phone, they may be more invested in "saying the right thing" than in sharing what they really think. This is especially true for hot-button issues such as gender and violence. Huntley and her team were acutely aware of this when they designed Gender Compass. "We created a gender equality bot," she says, "because we realised that people are scared to talk about this stuff." That made me think: would we see different results for the National Community Attitudes Survey if, instead of interviewing people over the phone, that survey was conducted online?

*

Changing attitudes on any subject is hard work. But changing people's deeply held beliefs about gender and violence is even more challenging.

Findings published last year help explain why this is so. They suggest that among male perpetrators misogynistic attitudes are not just loosely held beliefs that can be changed with the right education or "messaging," but are often deeply ingrained defence mechanisms against the traumatic impacts of their own childhood abuse, neglect and shame. What this means is that two known risk factors for perpetrating gendered violence – adverse childhood experiences and holding inequitable gender attitudes – are, unsurprisingly, closely linked. Exposure to violence and abuse in childhood and adolescence is a risk factor for developing anti-feminist attitudes *and* for perpetrating violence. It also found that child victim-survivors who go on to perpetrate violence in adolescence and adulthood hold on tight to these harmful attitudes and beliefs, even as the attitudes of their community improve.

That presents a clear dilemma for primary prevention, explains Kelsey Hegarty, joint chair in family violence prevention at the University of Melbourne and the Royal Women's Hospital: "Strategies to change gender attitudes in Australia are essential, but will be less impactful if kids are going home to households where their fathers are role modelling abuse and violence. In Australia, this is happening in *four in ten* households."

If persuasion and information are not sufficient to change these rigidly held attitudes or behaviour, is there another way?

*

Backlash to public health communication campaigns is common. Whether they target gendered violence, alcohol consumption or home energy usage, such campaigns are expected to generate a backlash – or boomerang – effect. I first heard about this phenomenon years ago during a visit to Safe Steps, Victoria's family violence crisis line, when CEO Annette Gillespie told me that when national advertising campaigns were running on gendered violence, they would get women calling in saying, "Can you get them to stop playing that ad on TV? Every time he sees it, he goes nuts." When violence-prevention campaigns provoke backlash, the horrible cost of that is borne by women and children.

But is this really inevitable? What if violence-prevention campaigns could be designed so they *didn't* provoke men who use violence? That's a question I started to explore back in 2021, when I was recording a podcast series on coercive control called *The Trap*. One evening, in the middle of another COVID lockdown, I spent two hours on Zoom with men who were participating in a behaviour-change program. During our wide-ranging conversation, I played for them a government violence-prevention ad that had aired recently in Victoria. It was a pretty typical example of prevention messaging, aiming to motivate men to call out sexist jokes and abusive behaviour. It goes like this: A group of male friends are sitting around a table in a pub when one of the guys, Johnno, gets a call from his girlfriend. He gives a knowing look to his friends, and says, "So here we go, it's Deb." Speaking abruptly to his girlfriend, he starts admonishing her – "I gave you enough money this week to get the – hey. Hey. I told you, you don't speak when I'm speaking." Johnno's friends look increasingly uncomfortable, but he's undeterred. "Seriously, do you, like, practise being this stupid?" Johnno ends the call and looks to his friends for validation. One says to him, "C'mon, Johnno, do you think that's funny? Cos that's not funny, mate." Johnno laughs and says, "It's just a joke, mate." But his friend stands firm. "It's not a joke, man." Then they all change the subject. The guy next to him gives him a slap on the knee and that's it. End of conversation.

Tyrone, twenty-nine, was blunt: "I get the point of the ad, but four years ago I would have been sitting on the couch and I would have been like, 'Tell that fucking person to shut the fuck up – don't tell him how to speak to his wife. I'll speak to my missus how I want to speak to my missus.'" Another participant was more sympathetic: "Part of changing society is making certain behaviours unacceptable. So from that perspective, the ad's coming from a positive place. But that man probably felt embarrassed. And, you know, anger and abuse come from a place of internal suffering. Even though we might think that shaming him is good, his internal suffering probably increased, and he might have gone home and [taken it out] on his partner. Shaming actually doesn't help. What we need to do is have really honest and frank and vulnerable discussions between men who can say, 'Hey, you know, we understand you might be suffering – this is how you can get some help, and here's something that enabled me to change.' But that's just not a discussion that's happening in in society, because it is all about shaming men. Everyone's acting like they're not part of the problem. No one's actually putting their hand up and saying, 'Hey, this is an issue I've had, too.'"

Whether or not all abuse comes from "internal suffering" is debatable, but what he was describing, essentially, was the difference between calling men out and calling them in.

One violence-prevention campaign, released in 2024, does exactly that: it calls men in. It's unlike any other I've seen. It's the first campaign to be run here in Australia by Matt and Sarah Brown, the New Zealand–based dynamo couple behind the global anti-violence movement She Is Not Your Rehab. Riffing on the line "not all men" – a notorious deflection used to shut down conversations about gendered violence – this campaign invites men to open up that conversation, and shows them how they can find their place in it. The ads are simple, a variety of messages on a green background: "Not all men break cycles. Will you?" "Not all men do better. Will you?" "Not all men heal. Will you?"

"Not All Men" is promoting SINYR's new app, innerBoy – a free thirty-day self-guided program that supports men to confront the harmful expectations of traditional masculinity, reflect on their behaviour, learn how to better self-regulate and begin to heal their own trauma. In New Zealand, more than 36,000 men signed up for innerBoy within an hour of its launch.

I was taken through the innerBoy model at a community hall in Campbelltown, down the road from the hospital where I'd met Theresa a few days earlier. As Samoan families gathered next door for an exuberant wedding, I sat in with Matt and Sarah as they led a workshop for mostly Aboriginal and Pasifika community leaders. This was not just a presentation on innerBoy – it was a live demonstration of what it takes to confront the most painful and hidden parts of yourself. Over those three hours, we told our stories, hugged, calmed our nervous systems, shared deep sadness and told profound stories of pain and healing. Some of it was deeply uncomfortable. Mostly, we arrange our lives to *avoid* feeling this vulnerable.

In all their work, Matt and Sarah model the kind of love and respect that underpins their global anti-violence movement. Matt, New Zealand–born to Samoan parents, brings a deep gentleness and cheeky humour, even when he's recounting his most painful childhood memories: his shorthand for conveying the violence and sexual abuse he grew up with is to say that when he and his siblings watched *Once Were Warriors* they thought it was a comedy. Sarah, a New Zealand Māori (Ngāpuhi/Te Rarawa) wāhine, brings care, compassion and formidable ambition. She is the engine driving their mission to "re-Indigenise" this work: "to use our own ways of connection and healing. We stand for ancestors of ours that have not been able to break cycles, who have passed on. And so when we do this *mahi*, this work, we collectively bring our people with us."

Messages from male ambassadors for "Not All Men" are supportive, appeal to notions of aspiration and male empowerment, and, perhaps most crucially, come from a place of shared experience. Fa'amanu Brown says, "Being a professional athlete in the NRL for over a decade I learnt firsthand that my mental fitness is equally as important as my physical fitness. I am proud to be a man in my family who broke the cycle of violence and I know innerBoy can help you too." Other promoted messages acknowledge the enormous personal pain and determination that goes into breaking cycles of violence – particularly the long journey of addressing childhood trauma. "People don't talk about how painful it is to come alive. To begin telling stories you were forced to hide. To start naming things that shut your heart off. To let anger and grief breathe. They don't talk about it because few do it. Shout out to my brothers willing to heal."

I thought back to how this campaign might resonate with a man like Tyrone, my guest on *The Trap*, who had experienced severe domestic violence as a kid and gone on to use coercive control against his wife. When he first entered the behaviour-change program, he "didn't understand emotions." "When I was growing up, I was taught, boys don't show, men don't show emotions," he said. "I still remember, clear as day. I jam fingers in a car door, I was four years old, we're at the motorbikes track and my stepdad looked at me, and like, we're with all the boys, and he gave me the look. He's like, *Don't cry now*. Four years old, I still remember it clear as day."

The poet Nayyirah Waheed illuminates the inner lives of so many men like Tyrone:

> there have been so many times
> i have seen a man wanting to weep but
> instead
> beat his heart until it was unconscious.

Tyrone beat his own heart until it became unconscious by using every drug he could get his hands on from the age of fifteen. In his twenties, he pulled himself together enough to don the "good guy" mask and project an image of success. "We'd go out, I'd have heaps of money, shout people drinks, shout people dinner, you know, 'Oh, he's such a good guy.' And I'd go home and my wife wouldn't put a glass away, or something wasn't in the right spot, and it's like you see on those ads: it'd be like, 'What the fuck, what's this doing here?' It's like, 'Fucking, if you hadn't done this, I wouldn't have done that.' Like, it's the title of your book." For Tyrone, hitting "that plateau of anger" made him feel at peace, because "Okay, I'm in control now … this is how I get things in life. This is how it works. And trust me, life *works*. I was making a lot of money. I had a really well-behaved girlfriend. And everything was rosy." Until it wasn't. "I didn't realise that I was quite abusive, really controlling and jealous." When that relationship ended, "Mum made me realise that my behaviour was unacceptable. And my wife made me realise that my behaviour was unbearable." Tyrone used coercive control because "it fed my ego, and it fed what I *thought* made me feel good. It was easy. That's why I did it." Connecting with his emotions – *coming alive* – and properly showing them "is the hardest thing I've had to overcome."

The ads we run, the messaging we use and the public discussions we have encouraging men to "embrace healthy masculinities" can make it seem like changing the way they think, feel and behave – that retraining their nervous system – is a simple matter of choice. But for many men, the decision to change is just the beginning of a long, hard and circuitous road. When I spoke to Tyrone that night on Zoom, he had been with the group for two years – the average men's behaviour-change program runs for sixteen to twenty weeks – and was still struggling to show vulnerability: "it's the hardest thing for me to actually grasp." His nervous system learnt early that vulnerability brought unbearable shame – rewiring that takes a lot of hard work, and time.

So how do we convince men like Tyrone to stop doing what's "easy" and instead do what's hard? How do we convince them that if they do the hard thing – the painful and difficult work of reconnecting with the scared little boy inside them – the benefits will far outweigh what they get from control, abuse and manipulation?

What if Tyrone had been taught about consent and respectful relationships when he was still a boy? Could better education have stopped him using violence? That's certainly the great hope. In the "river of prevention," schools are perhaps the most prized piece of "dry land." A captive audience, young minds at their most malleable – this is where violence can be stopped before it starts.

Our Watch CEO Patty Kinnersly singles out respectful relationships education as "one of the most crucial initiatives to eliminate this violence." "There is no space for culture wars on whether or not respectful relationships education should be urgently implemented," she wrote in an op-ed for *The Canberra Times* as homicides spiked in 2023. "Delay on this issue is leaving our young women experiencing violence, and in the worst cases, it is leaving them dead."

Only Victoria has mandatory Respectful Relationships education (in government schools), which it introduced in 2016. Teaching it is the job of staff teachers, and they do teach most of it, but for the topics on gender and power many call in external educators – "because it's far too controversial," says Deanne Carson, CEO of Body Safety Australia. Carson, a straight talker who has bottomless empathy for the kids she works with, is one of these external educators. What she's observed in Victorian schools since 2016 is that the new curriculum makes several things possible. For the teachers "who are champions for this work, and always have been, the curriculum gives them permission to do it with less personal risk." Other teachers will just "deliver the curriculum, which is more than they did before." Teachers who are openly sexist in front of their students and don't support this education "can at least now be directly addressed."

Under the guidance of Our Watch and others, Victoria has set out to nail the holy grail of prevention education: the "whole-of-school" model. Picture your local school. Now imagine if that school could be re-engineered into a miniature Iceland: a microcosm of gender equality, run according to gender-equal policies and procedures, staffed by teachers and leaders who openly reject rigid gender norms and champion equality and respect. This would be a whole other level of education for students – not just cognitive learning, but a revolution in their school's norms, modelled by the adults in charge. Now, with the picture of your local school as a gender-equal microstate, imagine how that example could radiate beyond the front gate, to influence the norms and attitudes not just of school parents but of the entire surrounding community. In a nutshell, that's the whole-of-school model. According to Our Watch, this holistic approach is "the single most important criterion for effective violence prevention and respectful relationships education in schools."

This vision – that re-engineered schools could spread gender equality to the broader community – is impressive and ambitious. The notion of this being realised in government schools across the state – and, eventually, across Australia – is probably easier to hold from a climate-controlled office in Melbourne's CBD. The real world, unfortunately, is a bummer. Government schools are facing enormous challenges, widespread teacher burnout and underfunding so chronic that many teacher are forced to buy their own classroom supplies. In this already strained environment, teachers – over 70 per cent of whom are female – are also coming up against what Monash researchers Stephanie Wescott and Steven Roberts have termed "a resurgent male supremacy." "While sexual harassment in schools isn't a new problem," they observe, "teachers are now describing something different: an escalating culture not only of sexual harassment, but of language and behaviours expressing belief in male superiority and other misogynistic views." In one national survey, teachers say they're being propositioned, threatened with rape, asked for nude photos, physically intimidated, and having their classes disturbed by young male students moaning sexually during class – even in primary school. The Independent Education Union in Victoria says violence from students against female teachers is also escalating. This has become more pronounced since COVID lockdowns, along with a noticeable deterioration in students' mental health and an increase in other problematic behaviours. That's something Daniel Principe, who delivers education to boys, has noticed "absolutely everywhere." "Attention spans, resilience, distractibility and more sexualised language. COVID was such an overdose of screen time and everything that goes with that, and we are now seeing some of the consequences of it."

Young people are already the highest-risk age group for sexual violence, but in more recent years the nature of that is changing. Every week in Victorian primary schools, an average of six incidents of child-on-child sexual abuse are reported to police. High-school students, too, are sexually exploiting fellow students – not just physically, but with new tech and deepfake apps. These stories are becoming legion – like the teenage boy at Bacchus Marsh Grammar, a regional private school in Victoria, who created and circulated the likenesses of fifty female students superimposed onto explicit sexualised images. "The photos were mutilated, and so graphic," said one of the mothers at the school. "I almost threw up when I saw it." When these incidents generate huge media attention, Carson gets phone calls from other schools reporting "copycat" incidents. "I think the media cycle and the use of social media has escalated the likelihood of copycat behaviours, and driven that down in age," she says.

This is why Carson gets frustrated with how prevention education is funded, as though it's a pure form of "primary prevention." "Every single classroom I go into, I have children who have been raped. I have children who have sexually abused other children. I have children living with family violence. I'm doing primary prevention in those spaces, but I'm also doing early intervention and response work." When schools confront the terrible occurrence of peer-on-peer sexual assault, they may call a service like Laurel Place. Kerinda is a mental health social worker, who for the past fifteen years has led Laurel Place's Reset program supporting young people who engage in harmful sexual behaviours. Once young people have offended against another child, the fallout is substantial: "they're often labelled as 'pedos' or sex offenders, so they're carrying a lot of shame." It's the job of Kerinda and the Reset team to help them address that shame and stop them using sexual violence.

Fifteen years ago, her referrals would mostly be from Child Protection for kids aged ten and older, who generally had complex trauma backgrounds and were living in out-of-home care. But now there are referrals for kids "as young as five or six, and they are coming from daycare and childcare centres." Kerinda says the big change she's noticed is that many of these kids haven't experienced sexual abuse themselves – instead, their harmful sexual behaviour appears to be linked to watching free online porn. "The porn these kids watch is traumatic – the images can be very violent and abusive – and it's also quite often extremely addictive." Exposure to this type of pornography, especially at such a young age, is not only traumatic in itself but can significantly impact sexual development and has been linked by other experts to the increase in sexual violence among children and young people. "We have a younger generation engaging in more sexual violence than previous generations," says Professor Michael Salter, the director of Childlight at UNSW. "When these children commit sexual violence, the acts are more extreme, because pornography has expanded their sexual vocabulary."

On average, young people are thirteen when they get their first lessons in sex and intimacy from free online porn. Almost half find it accidentally, via online searches or pop-ups. In much of this porn, degrading and painful sex acts are unremarkable, as are explicit racism and misogyny. In the majority of these clips, women not only go along with degrading treatment but are almost always grateful for it. Sahar, a young woman living in Tasmania, describes how that trope was at play when she was anally raped as a teenager: "I think he liked that it was painful for me. The next morning he told me to give him a blow job, and I did, and he slapped me while he was doing it. And I went, 'What the fuck?' And he was like, 'Oh, most girls like that,' like, 'Mature girls like that.'" In recent research from Our Watch, seven out of ten young people said the porn they watched often showed aggression and violence against women.

In parallel to these horror stories, of course, there is another truth – that this generation of boys and young men are "already way more switched on" than previous generations. "They blow me away with their insights," says Principe, whose passionate commitment runs through him like an electric current. "I have Year 7 boys popping their hand up and saying, 'Sir, that's objectification, that's sexualisation.' And I'm like, *How do you even know what that is?* So I get to see this insight and empathy from young people that's extraordinary … But I witness that in parallel with this increased callousness in some boys, a kind of performative toxicity. And what I'm hearing all around the country – even in the more progressive and alternative schools – is that these social norms, especially boys using violence, tearing down girls, making judgements based on skin colour and tearing other boys down – they are already manifesting by Year 6."

Given all this, it's perhaps unsurprising that the "whole-of-school" model – which seeks to inculcate gender equality and respect in teachers, students, parents and beyond – has had limited success. A multi-year evaluation found no evidence that Respectful Relationships education had any impact beyond the school. Parents, though supportive and interested, knew little of what was being taught. Teacher attitudes *were* improved – and there was data to prove that. But there was no data on the attitudes of students. Are the attitudes of Victorian high-school students improving? Are they getting worse? It's hard to say. We only get vague inferences, like "student attitudes towards gender and family violence were more varied [than teachers' attitudes] and have greater scope for change," and compared to primary-school students, influencing the attitudes and behaviours of high-school students was "more challenging."

But even more critically: is this education actually changing behaviour? Are there fewer students being victimised? Fewer students perpetrating? The evaluation doesn't say.

The whole-of-school model is best-practice for a reason. In Deanne Carson's work, educating *parents* is actually the most critical part, because children cannot – and should not – be expected to carry the burden of attitude and behaviour change alone, especially when their parents hold conflicting values. "Obviously, not all parents will be positively invested, especially those who intend harm," she says. "But loving parents who have not previously examined their parenting practices or their beliefs around gender norms engage earnestly in these conversations."

It's impossible to say whether a decade of Respectful Relationships education in Victoria has led to lower rates of gender-based violence among its young recipients. But in the classrooms Carson works in every day, she sees young people who are better informed and more empowered. "I see young people who are able to be more assertive and are better able to spot red flags and put in boundaries before things escalate to being unsafe. I also see young people who are much more able to intervene if they're noticing patterns of behaviour in their own friendship group." Not just young people who will call things *out*, says Carson, but those who will call things *in*. "I recently worked with some teens where there had been a sexual assault in the friendship group. The group actually sat down with the boy, and went, 'This is the impact of your actions, and this is what you need to do.'"

"We work in small groups and we work one child at a time. If a child has been abused, we give them opportunities to ask for help now, rather than when they're in their thirties or forties … opportunities to ask for help and to understand that not all relationships look like the ones they're living with. If a child is enacting sexual violence, we give them the opportunity to ask for help. For me, this work is not utopian. It is one child at a time, one classroom at a time, one school at a time, one town at a time."

*

Consent and Respectful Relationships education is set to be rolled out across the country this year, backed by $83.5 million from the Albanese government. What exactly will be taught remains a mystery – the guiding framework has not yet been released. The potential is great, but there are still live questions about whether such education can prevent violence – particularly sexual violence.

Four years ago, the federal government commissioned La Trobe University to do an "evidence review" of sexual violence prevention, to find out what – if anything – works. "We couldn't find one paper from Australia that told us anything about how to prevent sexual violence," says Professor Leesa Hooker, who led the research. "There's interventions and programs happening that have no evidence base behind them at all. That's a concern for the government now." Internationally, the La Trobe team found only a few programs that actually reduced sexual violence. These programs were based in tertiary education settings. The highest success rate was achieved by Flip the Script, a program directed at empowering and changing the attitudes and behaviours of young *women*. Over four three-hour sessions, it teaches women to identify when they're at increased risk of sexual assault, and to understand that the risk comes mostly from men they know, not strangers. It also teaches them verbal and physical defence skills to resist men trying to coerce or force them to have unwanted sex – because women who resist have a far greater chance of escaping an assault.

It's easy to say we should be teaching men not to rape, not teaching women how to avoid it. But wishful thinking doesn't stop rape. That's why University of Windsor professor Dr Charlene Senn developed Flip the Script in 2003 – because it was clear that efforts to stop men raping were either entirely ineffective or only marginally successful. She told *Ms.*, "There must be knowledge and tools [to] help [women] deal with this reality *now*, while other people are working on stopping perpetration and broader culture change."

Since the La Trobe review, an even more extensive meta-analysis of primary prevention education programs has found similarly disheartening results – described by two of America's leading sexual violence experts as a "damning wake-up call." The six-year project – a world first – scoured the world for every evaluation over a thirty-four year period (from 1985 to 2018). "The bottom line of these findings," summarised professors Mary Koss and Elise Lopez, "is that we have spent too much attention on changing knowledge, beliefs, and attitudes, which ultimately has not made a dent in sexual violence perpetration rates." Led by Dr Roni Porat, this enormous project did the analysis prevention practitioners had long been asking for. When I spoke to Dr Porat, she told me that, on releasing the paper, the team had been braced for a fierce debate. But apart from a smattering of attention from feminist media, there was very little interest. "Maybe it will take time, because we *are* going head on with the main approach to preventing sexual violence," concedes Porat. "We're saying, you know, 'You really need to rethink the strategy.'"

Reviewing evaluations from around the world (most of which come from the United States), Porat and her colleagues identified three distinct "eras" of prevention education: the first sought to educate teenagers about dating violence; the second aimed to enlist men as allies and increase their empathy for women and girls; and the third, the "bystander approach," sought to upskill students to intervene in risky situations and stand up to sexist comments. The bystander approach – which is particularly dominant across colleges and universities – has a familiar ring to it in Australia: prevention agencies and politicians commonly repeat the ethos that prevention is "everybody's responsibility," "The standard you walk past is the standard you accept" and it's "up to all of us" to call out our mates when we hear them being sexist or disrespectful. In an echo of the La Trobe review, this meta-review did not find that bystander interventions were successful in changing rates of perpetration or victimisation.

Virtually every intervention across the three eras rested on the same basic assumption: if beliefs and attitudes could be changed – and if rape myths could be dispelled – then ultimately a reduction in sexual violence rates would follow. What kind of "rape myths"? That women often make up false allegations, that victims are somehow "responsible" for their own rape (they were drunk, their skirt was too short, they led him on) and that rape only happens to certain kinds of women. This approach makes good sense: after all, studies frequently show that a greater acceptance of rape myths equates to higher rates of perpetration. However, though many interventions had changed students' self-reported beliefs, reductions in perpetration rarely followed. Their conclusion was shocking: "There is little to no relationship between changing attitudes, beliefs and knowledge and reducing victimisation or perpetration."

Only two interventions were given glowing reviews: Safe Dates and Shifting Boundaries. Both had not only improved student attitudes and knowledge but were shown also to significantly reduce the perpetration of psychological, physical and sexual abuse, their impact maintaining up to at least four years later. Safe Dates is also one of the few programs held up as proof in Australian reviews that education *can* lead to prevention. I was curious: what set these two interventions apart from the rest?

"The big difference I see is that these programs are more holistic," Dr Porat explains. Safe Dates, for example, not only runs a ten-lesson curriculum targeting a variety of things, including conflict resolution skills, it also includes behavioural components: students role-play confronting an abusive friend, and how to communicate effectively; they keep a "feelings" diary to learn how to recognise and handle their anger; they stage a theatre production, and they take part in a poster contest at the end, to help translate what they've learnt. Targeting behaviours is something Body Safety Australia's Deanne Carson talked about too. "There's so much conversation around masculinities programs and increasing empathy in boys," she says, "but it is not enough for us to just challenge attitudes and beliefs. We have to challenge *behaviour*, and we have to actually give them different ways of doing and being, instead of just saying, 'That attitude is wrong, the thing that you said in the classroom is wrong.' We need to help them understand *how* to do things differently."

In a curious twist, Shifting Boundaries, a high-school program based on Safe Dates, was also shown to reduce perpetration – but not through classroom learning. The violence was reduced only when changes were introduced at the "building-level" – such as increasing the presence of staff members and other surveillance in "hot spot" areas identified by students as "unsafe," introducing temporary school-based restraining orders, and revising protocols for how to respond to dating violence and sexual harassment. In other words, it targeted behaviour and the context it occurs in. Why wasn't the classroom learning enough to change behaviour? Porat says one notable difference was that Shifting Boundaries didn't include the role-playing and poster-competition components of Safe Dates, "which really brings students together and creates that sense of social norms being changed."

Other sexual violence experts who have analysed prevention education programs have observed the same phenomenon we see following awareness campaigns: the boomerang effect. After some programs – predominantly those that sought to enlist men as allies – young men surveyed afterwards showed even greater support for rape myths. Even more alarmingly, some even self-reported an increase in actual perpetration.

Why does some education make high-risk men even riskier? University of California professor Neil Malamuth – a well-regarded expert on the drivers of sexual violence, and an observer of the boomerang phenomenon – says you only have to look at the kind of psychological traits shared among high-risk men to see why they might resist typical prevention education. We're talking general antisocial tendencies, high degrees of narcissism, exaggerated entitlement, sexual arousal to force, and violence-condoning attitudes. As Malamuth wryly observes, when men like this are told they should be more empathetic towards women and girls, they are unlikely to be grateful for the correction; instead, they become defensive and resentful and hold on ever more firmly to their attitudes.

People tend to regard education as a benign product – the more education, the better. But education can be very powerful for good *and* bad. And the backlash to our messaging and education doesn't just happen inside people's minds – it manifests as real violence towards women and children. If we are going to mandate prevention education nationwide, we need to pay heed to the risk of a boomerang effect and how it can be avoided. That's why thorough and transparent evaluations are so important. They shouldn't just tell us whether the education is working, they should also test for whether it is doing inadvertent harm.

It's heartening to hear that some education programs can improve attitudes *and* lead to real reductions in violence. I hope we will see this success emulated here in Australia when Consent and Respectful Relationships education is implemented nationwide in 2025. Ultimately, though, until we see evaluations that transparently measure knowledge, beliefs, behaviours *and* violence, we cannot say for sure that this education will lead to a reduction in gendered violence.

In the office warrens of the federal government, disagreements over the National Plan's theory of change persisted for years. According to one insider, there were two family violence "camps" inside the Department of Social Services. In the area responsible for the plan, the "numbers people" in the research team questioned whether gender inequality and harmful gender norms and attitudes were both the central cause of family, domestic and sexual violence and the key policy lever to stop it. They believed this theory was incomplete and unsupported by the data. Of particular concern to them was the "Nordic paradox," so called because the Nordic countries – the most gender-equal countries on the planet – still have persistently high rates of gender-based violence (and intimate-partner violence rates even higher than the European average). They were also worried that a disproportionate focus on gender inequality and gender norms and attitudes had led to other significant risk factors, particularly child maltreatment and substance abuse, being deprioritised. Neglecting these factors, they believed, not only risked undermining the National Plan but put the lives of women and children at greater risk. According to this insider, other teams within DSS – those responsible for allocating funding and writing policy proposals – upheld the gender inequality theory as the "gospel truth."

These risk factors weren't being sidelined by accident. In fact, this was explicitly recommended by a consortium of Victorian gendered violence agencies, including Our Watch, in a submission to the Victorian royal commission in 2015. The submission was clear: alcohol abuse, poverty and violence against children should be seen as having "common cause" with violence against women, but a sustainable impact could only be achieved if "the bulk of investment and resources [are] dedicated to addressing the structural and normative gendered drivers of such violence."

Tension between the two camps in DSS eventually "came to a head," according to this insider, and the research team had to be moved to the other side of the office. Soon after, most of the research team either resigned or transferred out of the department (due also to concerns over leadership and workplace bullying). They were then replaced by new research staff who were "followers of the gender equality theory of change." Staff turnover is notoriously high at DSS, and since the change of government in 2022 there are newer staff in the department with their own misgivings about the plan's theory of change.

When your day job is to direct government policy on how to prevent violence against women and children, groupthink is especially dangerous – not least because it risks misdiagnosing the problem you're seeking to solve. For example, the Second National Plan briefly explains why domestic homicides had been steadily declining since 1989 until the recent upward spike. The thirty-year decline, it states, was the "result of increased awareness of family and domestic violence." But that's not right.

I asked one of Australia's leading domestic homicide researchers, Hayley Boxall, what the evidence says about the thirty-year decline in homicides. There are a few local contributors – some experts point to increased gun control, a decline in drinking, an ageing population – but in the literature Boxall has reviewed, "it's mostly due to improvements in medical technologies and improved response rates from ambulances. We're just much better at saving people's lives. The same decline has occurred internationally." It might seem churlish to fact-check a single sentence in the National Plan. But homicide reduction is one of its key targets, so a big part of its job is to guide federal, state and territory governments on actions that can help reduce domestic homicide by a quarter every year. What indication should they take from this explanation? That if they continue to raise awareness about gendered violence, fewer women will be killed?

Imagine if, in the strategy to reduce smoking, the dramatic decline in smoking rates was explained as the result of people learning that smoking was dangerous. That would certainly provide a good rationale for investing in awareness campaigns; in fact, the federal government would be wise to make awareness-raising the central prong of its smoking-reduction strategy. But those efforts would fail because, in reality, even when smokers learnt about the deadly risks of their habit, they kept smoking. To get Australians to stop smoking en masse, the federal government had to take drastic measures to make smoking almost *unavailable*. No smoking indoors, no smoking within four metres of a venue, no advertising, no fancy packaging (plus huge taxes). If awareness and rational thinking *were* enough to change people's behaviour, the Gillard government would not have been willing to fight one of the world's most powerful tobacco companies in court to legislate plain packaging. Moving the dial on intractable social problems is outrageously difficult. It requires governments to take on hard fights they generally prefer to avoid. To win those fights, they need to have the right evidence – and the social licence – to do so.

*

The DSS research team were right to be worried: by elevating some risk factors over others, Australia has pursued a prevention strategy that is dangerously narrow. Despite acknowledging harmful alcohol consumption and childhood trauma as "reinforcing factors," our prevention policy has largely neglected to address them.

For alcohol regulation advocates, this has been particularly devastating. "State and territory governments [have used] *Change the Story* to say they don't need to do more on alcohol regulation," says Caterina Giorgi, CEO of the Foundation for Alcohol Research and Education. "That is the unintentional impact of separating 'drivers' from 'reinforcing factors.' Whether it was intended or not, the framework is being used to diminish the role of the 'reinforcing factors,' and that has to be acknowledged."

Globally, alcohol abuse is one of the most significant predictors of violence against women and children. When men drink, their likelihood of using violence increases and the violence they inflict is more likely to be life-threatening. Radical interventions overseas have highlighted the strength of this connection: when the South African government banned alcohol during COVID lockdowns, violence against women *and* men reduced by 20 per cent, and during each week of the ban, there were seventy-seven fewer homicides, 790 fewer assaults and 105 fewer rapes. Similarly, a ban on alcohol in Bihar, India's most populous state, prevented 2.1 million cases of intimate-partner violence, according to modelling based on national surveys.

The reason we see such strong connections between alcohol and violence is that alcohol is a "whole-of-brain" drug that acts as a threat multiplier. As we get more intoxicated, alcohol produces a cascade of effects in our brain which make people already predisposed to being violent, controlling, jealous or aggressive even more dangerous. Intoxicated men, for example, get fixated on narrow issues, like perceived disrespect or suspicions of infidelity; become more willing to take risks; and are more easily angered by perceived constraints to their personal power.

Harmful alcohol use is associated with being both a perpetrator and a victim of violence. In sexual violence particularly, alcohol is not just a contributing factor. It can also be used as a weapon.

Two landmark surveys measuring rape on US college campuses (first in the mid-1980s, then in 2015) found that not only had the incidence of rape increased significantly between the two surveys, but the percentage of victims who said they were incapacitated by alcohol at the time of the assault also shot up from half in the 1980s to three-quarters in 2015. Nine out of ten men who admitted to sexual assault said they did it while their victims were incapacitated by alcohol.

"We do see, now, thankfully, a bit more discussion about how alcohol is used by offenders, which we didn't see in the past," says Sharna Bremner from End Rape on Campus Australia. "Educators will now talk about alcohol being used to facilitate assault, as opposed to, 'She drank too much, so what did she expect?' It's alcohol-as-a-date-rape-drug kind of thing. They're getting you drunk *on purpose*."

Substance abuse (alcohol and/or drugs) is also a known factor in 60 per cent of domestic homicides. In Hayley Boxall's review of almost 200 intimate-partner homicides, alcohol played the most definitive role in the 40 per cent of perpetrators classified as "persistent and disorderly" (defined as such due to their general level of dysfunction and frequent contact with the criminal justice system): 84 per cent were intoxicated when they killed their partner. In almost all cases, the decision to seriously harm the victim was made "instantaneously." Because they were pissed or high (or both), says Boxall, "they just didn't really have the executive functioning to pull themselves back, and go, 'I think I'm about to kill her, I'll stop.'" "There's clear evidence alcohol is associated with more severe cases of physical violence," Boxall adds, "and through systematic reviews, we know that women say that when he's pissed they are more likely to call the police, and we typically know that that's because they're more concerned for their safety."

Cathy Humphreys, one of Australia's leading experts on child abuse and gendered violence, says that while alcohol's role in domestic violence is a "national emergency," there has been "silence in this area." The silence is especially loud in our strategic plans: in the current Action Plan, for example, alcohol gets a single mention. In the National Drug Strategy, which targets drug- and alcohol-related harms, there is one mention of domestic and family violence and no mention of sexual violence. Feminist academic Dr Ingrid Wilson puts it plainly: "By not addressing alcohol as a factor, we are gaslighting women and telling them their lived experience doesn't matter."

Contrary to popular belief, alcohol-fuelled violence is not just an issue for women and children in disadvantaged areas: across Greater Sydney, the highest rates of alcohol-fuelled domestic violence occur in its *wealthiest* areas, led by North Sydney and followed by the Northern Beaches, Woollahra and Mosman. The lowest rates occurred in areas to the west: Canterbury-Bankstown, Cumberland and Liverpool.

Alcohol-fuelled violence is an urgent issue for children, too. A staggering one in six Australian children have experienced alcohol-related harm from adults, two-thirds of them from adults in their own home. Survivor advocate Kym Valentine recalls vivid memories of life as a little girl growing up with alcohol-fuelled violence, when she would hear the sound of screaming and shattering glass: "She perpetually holds her breath, hiding under beds, in closets, being thrown to the next-door neighbour in the middle of the night. She's told to run. This reality, one of fear – pure white fear – is one many children face, where the aim is to not set the bomb off." Valentine is now a research officer with Safe & Equal, Victoria's peak body for family violence services, and a passionate advocate for alcohol regulation. "For years," says Valentine, "we have told anyone who will listen that alcohol is a bomb, and it's intensifying our experience of violence. So what do we tell that little girl who hears the [online alcohol] delivery man pulling into the driveway? That we plan on getting back to her by the next generation?"

"When you ask people on the street, it shocks nobody that alcohol is significantly involved in family violence," says Giorgi. "It's only when we start to talk about theoretical frameworks that you hear people argue against this."

The semantic arguments on alcohol's connection to gendered violence are familiar to anyone doing advocacy or research. "I'm sure you've heard the mantra before," says researcher Ingrid Wilson. "Alcohol does not cause violence. Not every man who drinks is violent, and not every violent man is a drinker."

The argument over whether alcohol is a *cause* or a *correlation* is complex. To help understand why it is so heated, I called Annabelle Daniel, who chairs the NSW peak body for domestic violence organisations and runs Women's Community Shelters. Daniel, with her finely tuned bullshit detector, sardonic wit and fierce loyalty to victim-survivors, is a compassionate observer of this debate. She says the sector's reticence to be frank about the role of alcohol, and to support efforts to regulate it, is partly due to a fear of losing hard-won gains. For decades, it was widely believed that men's violence towards women was caused *primarily* by alcohol, anger issues and mental illness. While these are obviously critical risk factors, the disproportionate focus on them concealed the systemic nature of coercive control – the tactics of which are often unrelenting, and often persist post-separation, particularly through systems abuse. When feminists finally persuaded policymakers that men's violence was motivated by something insidious – their need for power and control – there was enormous relief: this was a big advance. But there is a lingering sense that this recently won territory must be fiercely defended, and to hold that ground, alcohol must be kept out of the picture. "It's like, *don't mention the war!*"

But for Daniel, it's time for that old conflict to end: "We can split these semantic hairs – cause versus correlation – until we're using a microscope, but the reality is that alcohol is significant for many victim-survivors. Some of them *only* experience physical and sexual violence, or identifiable coercive control, when their partner has been drinking. That is their reality. And if victim-survivors are saying they know they're going to cop it when the online alcohol delivery van pulls up at 11 pm, we need to respond to that."

The group best served by "splitting hairs" is, in fact, the alcohol lobby, which uses this semantic debate to argue against regulation. "There are submissions from the alcohol lobby to government that say, 'Alcohol does not cause violence,'" says Giorgi. Experts who have pushed back against this have been subjected to intense blowback. Giorgi says that over the past decade, FARE has been excluded from consultations on gendered violence, and explicitly instructed to caveat their advocacy with "Alcohol is not a cause but a contributor." "It's been difficult, because I expect that sort of response from alcohol companies and lobby groups, but not from people I'm trying to work alongside. We should be demanding more of our governments, not less."

Other once-outspoken experts found the tone of debate so punitive they withdrew altogether. Peter Miller, professor of violence prevention and addiction studies at Deakin University, has been silent on this for almost ten years. "My great frustration is that while they've been arguing semantics," he says, "many, many people have died, and things haven't got better. In fact, things have got worse." Miller speaks of a "lost decade" since the 2015 Victorian Royal Commission into Family Violence. When lawyers for the commission asked Miller to testify about the connection between alcohol and gendered violence, he initially turned them down. "I told the counsel assisting the coroner, 'Look, I've already been caned – I don't think I want to do this.'" But he changed his mind when the counsel assisting replied,

"The commissioners are really keen to talk to you, because we've spoken to 300 women and all of them talked about alcohol."

"Now I would like that on the record," says Miller, "because they so fundamentally failed those women. In fact, they made it even worse by allowing the government to completely bury it." The royal commission made only one recommendation on alcohol regulation: to consider family violence in Victoria's review of liquor licensing laws. When that review finally concluded, no changes were made to help reduce family violence. "I know [the royal commission team] were trying to do their best – and we all do – but it's so easy to lose heart when you see that happen," says Miller.

A decade later, South Australia is now holding its own royal commission and, once again, many victim-survivors have referred to the impact of alcohol.

Advocates aren't arguing for prohibition: they want common-sense changes, like a limit on the number of liquor stores allowed in a local area, a reduction in takeaway delivery hours, and restrictions on advertising. "We know, from a really large body of evidence, that if you reduce the availability of alcohol, you can significantly reduce violence against women, children and other men," says Miller. It also goes the other way: as Giorgi points out, when the NSW government extended alcohol takeaway and delivery sales by one hour in 2016, there was a significant increase in family violence assaults. Over thirty-eight months, this equated to an additional 1120 assaults across the state. "When every phone is a bottle shop and alcohol can be delivered within twenty minutes without any checks and balances," says Giorgi, "the risk of violence goes up."

Mainstream plans might have been silent on the connection between alcohol and gendered violence, but it's nothing new for Aboriginal advocates, who have been fighting this battle for decades. Nationally, Aboriginal and Torres Strait Islander people are the most likely to abstain from alcohol altogether, but those who do drink are more likely to drink to high-risk levels. The roots of this are no mystery: as the Victorian Indigenous Family Violence Task Force found, "alcohol and drug use masks many deeper issues such as loss of culture, identity, the effects of racism [and] powerlessness."

This combination can be catastrophic, especially for regional and remote Aboriginal communities, which is why alcohol regulation is recognised as one of the most powerful and immediate prevention levers governments can deploy.

Where this has been used effectively, the results have been astonishing. One of the earliest pioneers of this approach is former social justice commissioner June Oscar – a proud Bunuba woman from Fitzroy Crossing, in Western Australia – who, in the early 2000s, led a campaign to restrict the sale of alcohol in her hometown. After attending fifty funerals in eighteen months, Oscar and other leaders from the Marninwarntikura Women's Resource Centre decided to fight the "rivers of grog" fuelling catastrophic rates of family violence, child abuse, fetal alcohol spectrum disorder (FASD) and suicide in Fitzroy Crossing. "Alcohol was destroying our community, and it was affecting every aspect of life," Oscar later reflected. "We could not tackle educating people about their violent behaviours and their emotional triggers until we had restricted their access to alcohol." When they secured a ban on full-strength takeaway alcohol, the violence levels dropped dramatically: within six months, alcohol-related injuries in hospitals dropped by 85 per cent, and alcohol-fuelled domestic violence incidents dropped by 43 per cent.

Like most advocates, Oscar has never suggested alcohol restrictions will fix everything: they can't undo the ongoing harms of colonisation and they were "never intended to be a panacea for the enormous social disadvantages," which require "a long-term and permanent healing of the gaping wounds that arise from alcohol abuse and violence." But there is simply no other prevention measure that can replicate that kind of success.

With alcohol restrictions in place, the Marninwarntikura women turned their attention to tackling FASD, a neurodevelopmental disability that can include facial anomalies, violent behaviour, impulsivity, difficulty regulating emotions and problems with learning. FASD is a known risk factor for violence perpetration – it often starts young, with children attacking parents and carers, and if left untreated, their violence continues into adulthood. Fitzroy Crossing had the highest rates of FASD in the country, but "when the women learnt that their drinking was harming their babies, they started to change," Oscar says. The percentage of women drinking while pregnant dropped from 65 per cent in 2010 to 18 per cent in 2015.

Aboriginal advocates, experts and community members have long fought on the front line against alcohol companies – like the Aboriginal health workers and Elders in Darwin who spent five years fighting Woolworths and its plans to open a Dan Murphy's superstore within walking distance of a dry community. One of the most vocal and formidable opponents was Elder Helen Fejo-Frith, a role model and carer to hundreds of local kids over her lifetime: "We don't need a big mega store like that," she explained to media, "because it will just cause more violence, more people getting killed, people dying and children not being looked after." In the end, Woolworths abandoned its plans after a panel found it prioritised commercial objectives over the needs of the community and was insensitive towards local Aboriginal people.

It is broadly accepted among Aboriginal advocates that violence prevention must include alcohol regulation; many, including Professor Marcia Langton, made that clear in their testimony to the recent Northern Territory coronial inquest into the domestic homicides of four Aboriginal women. In her closing remarks, counsel assisting Peggy O'Dwyer did not mince her words. "Severe intoxication is a feature in each of these deaths … and in so many vicious assaults police are called out to in the Northern Territory … No serious policy to tackle violence can ignore the 'rivers of grog' that have fuelled it and have lined the pockets of those in the alcohol and gambling industries."

The alcohol lobby nationwide fights tooth and nail to prevent alcohol regulation. For twenty years, they spent millions just to delay the introduction of pregnancy warnings. "They fight hard against everything," says Giorgi. "They use it to send a warning shot: 'See, this is what we did to stop a label. Imagine what we'll do if you touch marketing or taxation.'"

The reluctance to highlight alcohol as a major risk factor is understandable. Though there are sore feelings on both sides of the debate, the only thing that matters now is what happens next. In the face of overwhelming evidence, and with such clear opportunities for prevention, it's time to stop the alcohol wars and apply the pressure where it should go: on the alcohol industry and the governments that regulate it.

*

If alcohol has been the elephant in the room, gambling is barely allowed inside the house. For years, anti-gambling advocates have been shouting into the dark about how gambling drives up rates of family violence. Where problem gambling is present, family violence is *three times* more likely. Poker machines, endemic across most Australian states and territories, are linked to the most extreme harms: not just family violence, but also child neglect.

In one recent study, victim-survivors described the myriad ways their partner's gambling was a terrifying accelerant to violence. Financial abuse – theft, fraud, creating debts in the woman's name, spending the family's income – contributed to a hothouse environment of secrecy and shame that was extremely dangerous. In one account, a man who had just lost big attempted to run down his partner in a car, pursuing her over their neighbours' front lawns. "For whatever reason, it was my fault," she said. "He'd done all his money … So it was, like, well, someone has to pay." When another woman confronted her partner about stealing her money to gamble, he "locked her and the children inside the house, removed the phones, and terrorised them before killing their pets."

Several of the victim-survivors interviewed had developed their own gambling addiction, because playing the pokies helped numb their pain and provided a place to escape their violent partner. "One of the reasons many women will gamble is to get out of the house. The pokies are a terrible place to go, but often they're the only place open. If you're trying to avoid a violent partner, the pokies are a place where you won't be approached or bothered, as long as you keep putting money into the machine," says Charles Livingstone, an associate professor in the School of Public Health and Preventive Medicine at Monash University. Livingstone is one of Australia's leading experts on gambling harms. He says the link between poker machines and family violence is stark: "We've known since almost forever that gambling and domestic family violence are very closely linked." Again, the story is writ large in the crime data: postcodes in Victoria with no electronic gambling machines (EGMs) have 20 per cent fewer recorded family violence or abuse incidents, and 30 per cent fewer domestic violence assaults, compared with postcodes that had seventy-five EGMs per 10,000 people. "Even after you adjust for factors like socio-economic disadvantage, the relationship is there – the more pokies there are, the more likely there is to be incidents of family violence," he says. "It's not a petty relationship. It's very real."

Gambling addiction – to poker machines and online gambling – is distinctly gendered: 14 per cent of men bet regularly, compared to 3 per cent of women. "The prime target for the gambling lobby is young men," says Livingstone, "and the way they do it is by promoting this hyper-masculine image of 'betting with your mates.' You know, the image of the guy sitting around with his male friends, placing their sports bets together. That's a million miles away from the reality for a lot of people, who are usually betting alone. It's not a pro-social activity."

The connection between big sporting events and higher rates of family violence is now well known – domestic violence assaults surge by more than 40 per cent on State of Origin nights, and on AFL grand final night Victoria Police report a 20 per cent increase in family violence. "We know that family violence and sport are inextricably linked," says Livingstone. "If you throw gambling into that mix and a few beers – both of which are heavily promoted by the AFL and NRL – you've got the money you've lost, on top of all the alcohol you've drunk, and all in a heavily masculine environment. That's a pretty volatile mix."

Perhaps that's why the tension between violence-prevention approaches is so vividly crystallised in a single image: AFL football players standing arm-in-arm in silence, right before kick-off, honouring the women whose lives have been stolen by other men. At nine AFL games in April 2024, teams observed a minute's silence, in the words of AFL CEO Andrew Dillon, "to make a strong stand and bring awareness to gender-based violence in Australia." As a gesture from the players, it was honourable. Seen through a primary prevention lens, it was priceless: male role models setting an example for the millions of boys and men across Australia who lionise them. But it's impossible to ignore the clear contradiction in the AFL's position. If Dillon truly believes that "the only acceptable rate of violence against women is zero," as I'm sure he does, then how does he explain the AFL's promotion of alcohol and gambling – products that are known to exacerbate violence? And why is the AFL lobbying governments to stop these products being regulated?

Gambling money pours into the AFL, not just through sponsorships and advertising but through a cut it receives from money gambled on their games: for every dollar made by corporate bookmakers such as Sportsbet, the AFL receives 10 cents. According to *The Age*, the revenue from that alone could have been as high as $40 million in 2022. Alcohol advertising is also ubiquitous: a 2019 FARE study found that seventeen out of the eighteen AFL clubs have commercial partnerships with the alcohol industry. Only one – the Western Bulldogs – did not. This gives alcohol companies valuable access to its next generation of customers, because it's only during sports broadcasts that alcohol advertising can be broadcast during children's viewing hours. This kind of exposure increases the likelihood of children drinking at a younger age, and that young people who already drink will imbibe at more dangerous levels.

After the 2023 Murphy Inquiry, led by the late Labor MP Peta Murphy, recommended a ban on gambling advertising, the AFL came out swinging: a ban would put its children's program, Auskick, at risk, it argued. Giorgi, whose organisation recently revealed that online gambling apps target social media users as young as fourteen, is explicit. "If the AFL and the NRL can go to governments and say, 'Don't regulate these harmful industries,' they might as well be working for those industries," she says. "They *are* working for them." On this point, anti-gambling advocate Tim Costello is fierce: "It seems the AFL and their ilk are all for tackling gender-based violence until it hits their bottom line."

It's not just the bigwigs at AFL HQ who rely on gambling revenue: a number of AFL clubs earn millions every year from poker machines they run themselves. Though the use of online gambling is rapidly increasing, poker machines still account for most gambling losses in Australia: $12 billion. (Online betting accounts for another $6 billion.) Globally, Australia is number one for the highest gambling losses: $1635 for every single Australian, every year. Half goes through the pokies.

In 2018, after a bombshell report by Charles Livingstone showed significant rises in family violence in areas hosting AFL-run pokie machines, AFL clubs suddenly started selling up their machines. For some clubs, that was reason enough to get out of gaming altogether. Today, only four Victorian clubs – Carlton, Essendon, Richmond and St Kilda – still run poker machines. The award for the highest number of poker machines goes to the Carlton Blues, which runs 300 machines across four venues in Melbourne.

Here again we see the tension between prevention priorities: while Carlton rakes in millions from gamblers, it also runs a high-profile gendered violence-prevention initiative, Carlton Respects, in partnership with Our Watch. Carlton's poker machines were a gift from its longtime powerbroker Bruce Mathieson, a billionaire pub baron nicknamed the "pokies king."

One of Carlton's biggest money-spinners is Club Laverton, in Melbourne's outer suburbs. Late one Monday night during a visit to Melbourne, I decided to check it out. After getting very lost – even with the aid of Google Maps – I finally found it: a single-storey venue attached to a small motel off the freeway. As I walked past the security guard and into the club, I was struck by the overwhelming presence of poker machines. No matter where you were in the small venue, the pokies were brightly visible and loud; no dividing screen here to conjure the possibility of doing anything else. You can get a meal in the restaurant area (roped off by 10 pm), but if you're not eating at Club Laverton you're here to gamble.

In my feeble attempt to blend in (just a regular night at the pokies with my notepad and pen), I bought a drink and sat at one of the sixty Aristocrat machines. I lost $5 in thirty seconds. When one young man in a business shirt and plaid pants left his machine momentarily, a woman stepped out from behind the bar to put a "RESERVED" sign on his machine. Soon enough he was back, and he was still playing when I left an hour later.

Leaving Club Laverton, one word kept repeating in my mind: predatory. Here, in this socially disadvantaged area, the Carlton Football Club has basically installed a cash machine to withdraw millions of dollars every year from the local people who can least afford it. In 2022–23, gamblers fed $19,709 every day into the pokies at Club Laverton, amounting to almost $7.2 million for the year. Across all four of its clubs, Carlton's pokies revenue exceeded $20.5 million last year.

"It's completely unconscionable for Carlton to purport to be concerned about violence against women while they have this massive poker machine operation," says Livingstone. "It's shameful. We know exactly what we need to do: reduce accessibility. Same with alcohol. If you reduce accessibility, you reduce demand."

A CHANGE OF PLAN?

I developed my own misgivings about Australia's approach to prevention after reading the First National Plan. I questioned the strategy at length in my 2019 book, *See What You Made Me Do*, because, among the hundreds of interviews I conducted over several years, I often heard the same misgivings from academics, bureaucrats and frontline workers: many believed the strategy pursued by Our Watch and other government prevention agencies was too abstract and disconnected from the front line; that it did not reach the boys and men it needed to, and at worst was actually *promoting* backlash. Many were – and still are – afraid to say so openly; some for fear of losing funding, others for fear that challenging a powerful orthodoxy could risk relationships and even lead to reputational damage. Several analogised this trap to the Emperor's New Clothes – in which people are afraid to criticise something because everyone else seems to think it's wonderful.

The only senior academic I could find who would speak publicly was Professor Michael Salter. His opinion was particularly valuable because he wasn't some tetchy outsider but a leading expert on gender-based violence on the National Plan advisory group. When I interviewed him in 2018, Salter was already exasperated. Prevention approaches were, he said, "dangerously missing the mark": "Treatment based on these liberal feminist principles is not working. It's not working! At this point, why on earth wouldn't we swivel to recognise that these guys have an inner world?"

In the years since, questioning the dominant prevention paradigm has become even more difficult. Several leading researchers, for example, have told me that when they presented evidence that contested parts of *Change the Story*, they were abruptly shut down. "Frameworks are useful, but they are not written in blood and stone," says Annabelle Daniel. "The only way to do prevention well is to listen to victim-survivors, partner with the front line and get among the grassroots. This is not something that should be churned out in an academic factory."

No area of public policy is a protected species. Open debates are a necessary, albeit difficult, way to improve theory, policy and practice. And questions about prevention approaches aren't being raised only in Australia. Globally, data from the World Health Organization shows that rates of intimate-partner violence among young women aged fifteen to nineteen are already incredibly high, at 24 per cent. The global prevalence rate for *all* women over fifteen is only 2 per cent higher – 26 per cent. This means that teenagers who have just started dating have already accrued almost the same experience of intimate-partner violence as women who've been in relationships for decades.

In a 2023 paper, Spanish researchers analysed this increase and asked: "Is prevention failing?" "The problem is not just this high rate of violence among young people," says one of the paper's co-authors, Professor Enrique Gracia. "The problem – hidden in plain sight – is that we don't know how to prevent it." Gracia, a professor of social psychology at Spain's University of Valencia, has been particularly well known in the prevention field since 2016, when he co-authored "Intimate partner violence against women and the Nordic paradox." This was the first paper to highlight those counterintuitive statistics from Nordic countries that showed surprisingly high rates of gender-based violence. Shockingly, these statistics showed that, compared to the European Union average of 22 per cent, around 30 per cent of women in Denmark, Finland, Iceland, Sweden and Norway had been subjected to physical or sexual violence from an intimate partner. Though the Nordic paradox was evidenced by one Europe-wide survey, other country-wide surveys have since confirmed the same high levels of gender-based violence, including sexual assault.

The Nordic paradox raised serious questions about a truism that drives prevention efforts globally: that countries with higher rates of gender equality have lower rates of gender-based violence. Unsurprisingly, it provoked an intense debate. "When 'The Nordic paradox' went out – that was really a blow-out," laughs Gracia. "People were writing papers against it, arguing, 'No, no, no, this is wrong. There must be something wrong with the numbers.' Or, you know, explanations like, *Swedish women talk more freely about* it. That's not even true – there's higher rates of reporting to police in Spain, where violence rates are much lower than in Sweden. But of course, they have to find something to protect their approach," he says. "Nobody has ever denied that gender equality, gender norms, sexist attitudes are a risk factor. Of course they are important, and we should keep trying to change them – but right now, we don't know how to do that. It's like cholera – we know the bacteria that's related to it, but we still haven't created a vaccine for it."

It's a confusing picture, because the evidence from various countries is inconsistent. Evidence from a study in Nicaragua, for example, shows that a strong feminist movement – focused on law reform, service provision, awareness-raising and gender norms – was at least partially responsible for a massive reduction (over twenty years) in rates of physical intimate-partner violence (though no such reductions in *sexual* violence). Results like these should be analysed closely because, as the study authors commented, "the evidence base on how to transform gender norms and prevent VAWG [Violence Against Women and Girls] on a large scale through structural interventions remains limited."

Gracia says that efforts to improve gender equality and social norms should continue and must be evaluated to see if they are having the desired effect. "And of course," he says, "you have to prevent violence from the very outset. The younger you start, the better: preventing violence in childhood, preventing child abuse. My PhD was in trauma treatment, and a lot of violence stems from trauma. But that's like the elephant in the shop – nobody wants to talk about that."

*

In 2023, you could barely go a few days without hearing about another man murdering a woman. In just one fortnight in May, men allegedly killed three women: Tatiana Dokhoratu in Sydney, allegedly murdered by her estranged partner while her three-year-old son was at home, and whose parents found out about her murder on social media. Monique Lezsak, stabbed to death in a "violent and frenzied" attack by her bodybuilder boyfriend Sven Lindemann as her ten-year-old daughter fought to protect her, desperately wrestling knives off him; and Kristy Armstrong, remembered as a best friend to her three daughters, killed when her ex-partner deliberately drove his ute at 140 kilometres per hour towards her sedan – two of her girls were in the car with her. Three women murdered, and six children who would now have to navigate life in the shadow of this violence, without their mothers to love them.

As the murder rate spiked across the country, news was also coming out of the high-profile coronial inquest in the Northern Territory examining the murders of four Aboriginal women: Kumanjayi Haywood, a much beloved daughter burnt alive by her partner of twenty years as she hid in a bathroom; Ngeygo Ragurrk, an Aboriginal ranger, knowledge-keeper and carer to many in her community, who was killed by her partner in a brutal attack on Darwin's Mindil Beach; Kumarn Rubuntja, a well-known and loved anti-violence advocate whose partner hit her deliberately with his car; and Miss Yunupiŋu, remembered as a smart, intelligent, caring and beautiful young woman who had been trapped in a thirteen-year cycle of leaving and returning to her partner, who eventually stabbed her to death. All four women were repeatedly failed by police and other institutions they reached out to for help.

Across Australia, each reported murder fed a growing sense of horror and outrage. But when journalists sought answers from politicians and prevention leaders on how to stop the killings, the answers were often jarringly banal: *We all have a role to play in ending gendered violence, and we can do that by challenging harmful norms and calling out our mates when we hear them "disrespecting women."* Each time a woman or child was murdered, I felt a gnawing sense of urgency. If it's *everybody's* responsibility to prevent violence, where does the buck stop?

As the murder rate climbed, I was undergoing radiation and chemotherapy for recurrent brain cancer. Confronting mortality can do wonders for your perspective; for me, the long, sleepless nights during treatment brought my frustrations over prevention into sharper focus. So, for what it was worth, I decided it was time to say the quiet part out loud. When I asked Michael Salter to do it with me, he immediately agreed.

"Over the past ten years, I've been told on multiple occasions not to talk about childhood trauma and its link with men's violence against women," says Salter, explaining why he felt motivated to speak again on this. "Services doing great violence-prevention work with traumatised boys can't get government funding, because their way of doing prevention doesn't square with the priorities in *Change the Story*. So instead, they have to rely on money from philanthropists. Outside of a very specific conversation about Aboriginal and Torres Strait Islander communities, there's been virtually no role for childhood trauma in prevention work. As long as we continue to obscure the central role of childhood trauma and relegate it as a less important 'reinforcing' factor, we are never going to see the level of investment we need in child wellbeing and safety."

In July 2023, between my chemo treatments, he and I nervously stepped up to the lectern at a coercive control conference in Sydney and presented *Rethinking Primary Prevention*. In it, we argued – as I have in this essay – that across several metrics Australia's prevention strategy is failing, and that while Australia is to be commended for leading the world in funding and developing primary prevention, we are "not world leaders in *actually* preventing violence." We called on governments to develop a broader appreciation of the many risk (and protective) factors for gendered violence, and to lean into largely ignored opportunities for prevention: to better prevent child maltreatment and help those harmed to recover; to regulate harmful industries, including alcohol, pornography and gambling; to make courageous structural changes that would support women to live independently; and to bolster consequences (of various forms) for adult perpetrators and the government systems that protect and enable them.

In February 2024, Prime Minister Anthony Albanese signalled a significant policy shift: "We must face up to where we are falling short and look for new ways to do better … We must recognise that gender equality – while essential – does not safeguard against violence on its own. Indeed, even nations that lead the world on measures of gender equality are dealing with their own shocking rates of violence … Addressing family violence cannot begin and end with efforts to achieve gender equity or economic equality. We have to go deeper than that," he told an International Women's Day parliamentary breakfast in February 2024. "We need to put the focus on prevention and we need to do that in new ways … Because all the data tells us that men who perpetrate violence as adults are more likely to have experienced violence as a child. We know that's not the reality for everyone. Ending violence in a generation means making sure it's not the reality for anyone."

To those closely watching this debate, the prime minister's intervention was significant and brave. But journalists barely noticed it, because in general they don't pay close attention to this area of policy (nor do any of the many think-tanks that analyse other areas of policy). Instead of reporting this bold policy shift, the media focused mostly on the PM's exhortations to men to "step up."

Two months later, when we published *Rethinking Primary Prevention* online, the response was overwhelming. It made front-page news, provoked thoughtful responses from advocates across the sector and was discussed by a dozen of Australia's leading columnists. Annabelle Daniel recalls the response of some of her frontline colleagues: "I spoke to more than a few people across the sector who said, *It's really good that we're talking about this.*" As expected, there was also sharp critique, particularly from practitioners and academics aligned with primary prevention agencies in Victoria (the state most heavily invested in the approach we criticised). I could devote several pages to the heated back-and-forth that followed – bruising for all involved. Public debates on sensitive issues can be extremely difficult, but we should always do our best to constrain our disagreements to the level of ideas.

In May, urged on by angry Australians in their thousands who rallied in cities and towns at the No More! protests, and by national crisis talks convened by Domestic, Family and Sexual Violence Commissioner Micaela Cronin, National Cabinet convened a special meeting and commissioned a rapid review to identify targeted, evidence-based ways to prevent violence. (I was appointed to the expert panel, along with five others.) Given the diversity of positions, the money involved and the lives at stake, the politics of the review – its members, its scope, its very existence – were precarious. The review would be convened by three powerful public servants: Domestic, Family and Sexual Violence Commissioner Micaela Cronin, director of the Commonwealth Office for Women Padma Raman, and secretary of the Department of Social Services Ray Griggs. The focus was squarely on finding ways to stop male perpetrators, so the panel was split equally between women and men, including Wiradjuri man and former Victorian LGBTIQA+ Commissioner Todd Fernando. There should also have been an Aboriginal woman appointed, and the failure to do that – considered even more offensive in the aftermath of the failed Voice referendum – was rightly called out.

After an intensive twelve-week process, the panel suggested substantial reforms, such as mandated training for GPs and psychologists (the professionals to whom victims and perpetrators are most likely to disclose); regulations for alcohol and gambling (including a ban on gambling ads); independent oversight for police to increase accountability and improve responses; a halt to perpetrators weaponising government systems like child support, family law and Centrelink; protecting victim-survivors from tech-facilitated abuse; strengthening women's economic equality; conducting an urgent inquiry into domestic violence-related suicide; and prioritising the safety and wellbeing of children and young people. Topping the list was an explicit recommendation that governments give priority to the experiences and needs of Aboriginal and Torres Strait Islander peoples and support them to lead their own prevention efforts.

The panel was recommending a new way of looking at prevention altogether, and thus also recommended that Australia's prevention framework, *Change the Story*, be independently reviewed.

National Cabinet responded to the review with a much-needed $800-million increase in funding. There was a raft of commitments, including an immediate audit to identify how Commonwealth systems are weaponised by perpetrators; $80 million to expand support for child victim-survivors; and a commitment from states and territories to review how alcohol laws affect family and domestic violence victims, and propose reforms. That final recommendation on alcohol was, according to insiders, extremely hard-won, requiring strong negotiating by the prime minister.

So, given this much progress has already been achieved, why am I even writing this essay? Isn't the battle already won?

Not even close. There's been no response yet to many of the recommendations, including the one to review *Change the Story*. Aside from the announced discrete packages of funding, there's little proof yet that governments are willing to substantially redirect their approach – let alone truly grapple with what that would require.

"We've got systems that are like a huge, upturned bowl of jelly. 'Oh, things are terrible, we need to reform. Yes, yes, yes – let's talk about prevention and early intervention.' You see the jelly wobble, it looks like things might change, but every time you prod it, the jelly just really wants to wobble back into its old shape," says Natalie Siegel-Brown, an unapologetically blunt ex-bureaucrat turned watchdog, who has spent the past twenty-five years in senior private sector and government roles. Her expertise is vast, ranging across domestic and family violence, youth justice, child protection, elder abuse and Indigenous affairs. "In government, our starting presumption to paradigm-upsetting reform or change can often be 'no.'" For an optimist, talking to Siegel-Brown is like taking an ice bath – invigorating *and* uncomfortable. "Where is the theory of change here?" she asks. "We know that the most common background for perpetrators is adverse childhood experiences, but we exclude the science on the connection between childhood trauma and perpetration from the mainstream discussion. We have to ask ourselves: what is the attitudinal shit in Australia that is blocking us from listening?"

Despite the pressing need for greater understanding of what drives men to perpetrate gendered violence, there's precious little research on it – especially in Australia. But the few studies we *do* have justify Siegel-Brown's frustration. "When you look at these men's histories, trauma is just really bloody common," says the ANU's Hayley Boxall. "For the guys in our homicide sample, more than 50 per cent had some form of really significant childhood trauma."

As I mentioned earlier, Boxall recently led research into "perpetration pathways." Using crime data, sentencing remarks and coronial findings, she wanted to identify the common life trajectories shared by men who murdered their intimate partners. The vast majority – 84 per cent – fit into three distinct pathways: fixated threat (33 per cent) – highly controlling, typically middle-class men who had low levels of contact with the justice system; persistent and disorderly (40 per cent) – jealous and controlling men with complex trauma and other health problems, and significant histories of intimate-partner violence; and deterioration/acute stressor (11 per cent) – typically older men with significant emotional, mental and physical health problems, whose abuse was triggered by a deterioration in their health and wellbeing. Although each pathway was distinct, they shared a list of common features, including increased consumption of alcohol and drugs, a perceived loss of control over their victim, and the offender's own history of abuse growing up. "And we're talking about the sort of trauma that would make anyone go, 'Wow, that's really messed up,'" says Boxall. "Things like systemic sexual abuse, having a parent die, having a parent threaten to suicide in front of them." In a "large number" of cases featuring migrant men, it was exposure to war and conflict. "I think we need to have a broader lens when we're thinking about trauma – there's other kinds of horrendous trauma these blokes have experienced."

While gendered drivers are clearly part of a "constellation of risk factors," Boxall says, the evidence on how they influence perpetrators is limited. "Attachment is actually one of the most helpful lenses we have at the moment to explain perpetration, because it helps us understand how the individual relates to other people in their social orbit," she says. What Boxall is referring to here is attachment theory, which shows how our bonds with early caregivers shape how we trust, communicate and resolve conflicts in our later relationships. If a person has "secure attachment" – because their caregiver was loving and responsive – they bring that intrinsic feeling of safety and confidence into their relationships. If a person's caregiver was inconsistent, neglectful or abusive, they may develop "insecure attachment"; later in life, their "attachment style" may be more "anxious" (craving intimacy, but fearing abandonment) or "avoidant" (prone to being distant emotionally and needing independence). There's a lot more to attachment theory, but that's it in a nutshell. "Your primary attachment figure as a child is your parents (or carer); your next primary attachment figure is your intimate partner. So if your attachment style is messed up because of what you experienced as a child, you're going to carry that into your subsequent relationships."

*

Reader, it's my duty to pause here and inform you that we are right now standing in the middle of a fifty-year-old turf war. On either side, we're flanked by two armies: strict adherents to the "feminist" model on one side, and loyalists of the "psychopathology" model on the other. These were the two camps that fought during Victoria's royal commission, in fierce disagreement over what causes gendered violence and how best to stop it. *Change the Story* was supposed to end the war once and for all, but instead of making the compromises necessary for a lasting peace, it simply handed victory to one side. So what do these two sides believe, and why are they so opposed?

Defenders of the psychopathology model insist that perpetrators are aberrant, and that their behaviour is rooted in mental illness, substance abuse and childhood trauma. Many on this side have historically dismissed notions of gender and patriarchy as an unnecessary distraction. In other words, from a strict psychopathology perspective, only "sick" individuals would harm people they claim to love.

Crusaders for the feminist model have spent the past fifty years warring against the defenders of psychopathology – they see it as a Trojan horse for protecting the patriarchy. From their point of view, making perpetration an "individual" problem will allow governments to ignore the broader cultural influences – misogyny, gender inequality, racism, homophobia, etc. – that make men feel entitled to dominate, discredit and disregard women. In *See What You Made Me Do*, I described the "feminist" model:

> If an abusive man is a room, then toxic gender attitudes and beliefs – like "women belong in the home," "real men don't cry," "women often make up false rape reports to punish men" – are the floor. The abusive man's "floor" may have a lot of heavy furniture on it – alcoholism, drug addiction, mental illness, child abuse, unemployment and so on. The furniture in each abusive man's "room" makes it look unique, and sometimes the room is so crowded you can barely see the floor. But that floor – the gender stereotypes that form the foundation of this man's expectations and behaviour – is still there. It's what all that furniture is sitting on.

Australia's prevention strategy advises governments to spend more time and money rebuilding the foundations of the house, not just replacing the broken furniture. I promise not to torture the house metaphor for much longer, but if you're renovating a house, you can't just leave the furniture there and rip out the floor – you need to attend to the foundations *and* the furniture.

This essay is arguing for a properly negotiated peace, and a lasting end to the war. There are many practitioners who occupy *both* sides – and bringing the others closer together should be a key priority. Two things can be true at the same time. As the more recent version of *Change the Story* makes clear, Australia's prevention strategy should be alive to how gendered violence is driven by power imbalances – from gender inequality to homophobia, racism, economic inequality and ageism – as well as by suffocatingly narrow models for masculinity. But it must *also* strive to stop violence passing from one generation to the next, which requires a much stronger focus on preventing child maltreatment, helping children and victimised parents recover, placing more limits on harmful industries, helping men who are willing to do the work to heal, and keeping women and kids safe from the men who won't. It's only by integrating both viewpoints – feminism and psychopathology – that we can start to truly comprehend the phenomenon of men's violence against women and children and find effective ways to stop it.

For the past twenty-five years, that's what Natalie Siegel-Brown has been trying to do. In the early 2000s, she was an early family violence pioneer in government who helped to translate the feminist analysis – that men do it for power and control – into policy and practice. Over time, however, Siegel-Brown found that this analysis, while meaningful, also raised more questions: "Where does his need for power and control come from?" This is a question I've also been interrogating for years – it couldn't *only* be male entitlement: in situations of intimate-partner violence, men go to such extremes they end up ruining their own lives. As homicide offenders, they are also unique: no other category of murder so commonly ends with the offender taking their own life.

That need to go deeper led Siegel-Brown to study neuroscience. Today, she teaches on the connection between trauma and violence – mostly overseas, where the appetite for it is much stronger than in Australia. She says it's past time for Australia to pay attention to the "good strong bloody neuroscience" on the connection between trauma and violence. As she lays that out for me, she speaks quickly and passionately – like someone who knows that everything is at stake and there is no more time to lose. Much of her explanation can be conveyed through a single image: the brain MRI of a traumatised three-year-old. In this image, she explains, you can see that the limbic system or "back brain" – which governs the fight/flight/freeze response – is massively *over*developed. Inversely, the frontal lobes or "front brain" – the part that governs executive functioning, brings perspective and helps you regulate otherwise overwhelming emotions – is *under*developed. "In a healthy child," she says, "it's the reverse."

When children grow up with complex trauma, the physical changes in their brain set them up for a nervous system that is hypersensitised to threat and is constantly in fear of where the next attack is coming from. That kind of uncertainty is obviously intolerable, so these kids may disrupt calm situations in an attempt to gain some kind of control over it. "The common thing you hear from their adult carers is, 'I don't get it – when things are calm, this child loses their shit,'" says Siegel-Brown. "That's because they feel so out of control and hypervigilant [that] they're always braced for the next blow-up. If they set off the fire, then at least they're in control of when and how it happens."

Some of these children will outgrow this. But for others, this deeply ingrained need for control can manifest in other ways. "If you've got this brain that's hypersensitised to threat – one that expects to be harmed – and you don't help it to recover, you can have an adult who is constantly seeking power and control over their environment. They develop an insatiable appetite for it, which can evolve in a whole range of behaviours, including coercive control and sexual violence." This echoes what I've seen in the research: when you throw gender roles and a bit of biology into the mix, you end up with a scenario where men are more likely to seek control using violence against others. Women may also translate a need for control into violence – especially towards those over whom they have the most power, like their children – but that's not as common. They are more likely to internalise their need for control, and harm themselves through perfectionism, overwork and anxiety.

Despite the established evidence connecting childhood trauma to gendered violence, Siegel-Brown can still feel apprehensive about raising it in Australia. "I'd be treated as a heretic if I came out right now and said, 'Let's have a look at the profile of the childhood experiences of perpetrators and ask what that tells us about childhood recovery,'" she says. "But it's completely unsurprising to me that we have such a high prevalence of childhood maltreatment in Australia *as well as* high rates of family violence. I see maltreatment as the key precipitator of the power and control behaviours of perpetrators. Of course many victims of child neglect and abuse never go on to become perpetrators of family violence. But we know the reverse is often the case; many perpetrators have experienced emotional and/or physical neglect and abuse."

She says this also explains why, no matter how hard we try, we simply won't change some people's rigid attitudes with awareness and education. "Why do we find it so hard to change these rigid attitudes around things like misogyny? Because perpetrators who have traumatised backgrounds find safety in rigidity and prejudice."

Professor Michael Salter says it's for this reason that Australia must pivot towards a trauma-informed approach to prevention. "Misogyny is a very effective defence mechanism for boys and men who've been ashamed and humiliated in the past. It is a short-cut away from fear – a way to feel powerful and proud at the expense of women. I'm not saying all misogynists are traumatised, but those who really lean into misogyny, racism and homophobia tend to be more traumatised than other men. Our interventions, quite understandably, attack and disparage misogyny – it's a very unlikable phenomenon. But if you're going to remove a maladaptive defence mechanism like misogyny and say, 'You're a bad person for thinking that way,' you need to provide these young men with a pathway to thinking differently. How do we support them to think and feel differently, so that misogyny is not something they reach for when they feel vulnerable or anxious or embarrassed?"

The evidence is clear: Australia needs a prevention framework that explicitly recognises the strong influence of childhood trauma on perpetration. "If you took a public health approach to domestic and family violence," says Siegel-Brown, "I can guarantee you that while gendered attitudes would be on the list, they would not be sitting alone at the top. If we did this right, we would reduce spending over time."

It is the purpose of this essay to amplify the many voices – experts, frontline workers and victim-survivors – urging governments to transform Australia's prevention strategy. The evidence is clear: unless governments do everything in their power to provide safety and recovery for children and young people, the violence will only get worse. In the words of Australia's National Children's Commissioner, Anne Hollonds, "Children are the prevention opportunity that has been ignored." She is not being hyperbolic. In the years we've spent trying to change young hearts and minds, we have almost completely neglected to provide systems that would actually keep them safe. Imagine if we taught young people the truth about what could be waiting for them, if they go looking for help …

Under eighteen and using violence? Sorry, there's almost no help for you, unless the police catch up with you – then, if you're older than ten, we can put you in jail. Fleeing family violence on your own? Too bad, there's no family violence refuge for you – but you can get a bed in a youth refuge for a few weeks. After that, hopefully someone will let you sleep on their couch – if not, you'll have to sleep on the street (sorry if you have to trade "survival sex" for a bed). If your victim parent does manage to leave, the Family Court may get to decide where you live – but don't worry, with luck you'll get a judge who understands violence and coercive control, and they won't order you to see or live with the parent who's abused you. But if you *are* ordered into that abusive parent's care, don't try to run away, because a court recovery order could set the Australian Federal Police after you. And if your mum is struggling after living under the yoke of constant threat and degradation, Child Protection can help out – only they can't really offer her much help, and they may just scare her by threatening to take you away. If you do get removed, maybe you'll end up with someone who gives you the care you need – or maybe you'll end up living in a hotel room for months on end, supervised by staff from labour-hire companies working eight-hour rotating shifts.

If we told young people what kind of "help" we might be offering them, what might they have to tell us about "respect"?

*

Twenty-one-year-old Conor Pall spends most of his waking hours trying to persuade policymakers to respect and respond to children and young people. He knows what it's like to be ignored and further endangered by systems that should be there to keep kids like him safe. Pall has strong "eldest son" energy, and in just a few short years his quiet drive and determination have helped him become one of Australia's most recognisable advocates for young victim-survivors. For Conor, there's an acute irony to this: "We are consulted more often than we are supported."

In his travels across his home state of Victoria – famed for its nation-leading response – Conor has seen firsthand just how barren the landscape is for young victim-survivors who need help. In regional areas such as Mildura, the cross-border town where Conor grew up, the waitlist for children and young people to get therapeutic support is over a year. "Those young people have made a disclosure, they're asking someone to help them deal with the ongoing risk they're facing, and the door is slammed in their face. What are they supposed to do?" Services are so scarce that when one does become available it's quickly overwhelmed. "Six months ago, I was in Ringwood [25 kilometres east of Melbourne's CBD] and a family violence service opened their books to a therapeutic healing and recovery counselling service for children. On day one, they got fifty referrals and had to shut their books."

The mainstream family violence system is built for women and their children; if teenagers aren't with a protective parent willing and able to seek support, they rarely get help. "I hear about children and young people calling specialist family violence services saying they're at high risk, and they're told, 'Call Kids Helpline.' *Kids Helpline*. Like, what the fuck?"

Kids Helpline may be great for kids who need counselling, but it can't provide the urgent, practical help young victim-survivors often need.

When he was a young teenager, Conor tried calling a mainstream family violence service for help: first they asked him if he was the perpetrator, a term he'd never even heard before. When he told them *he* was the victim, he was told he couldn't access the service because he didn't have a protective parent ready to seek help. Stranded, Conor struggled with addiction, using alcohol to "numb the pain." It wasn't just the trauma Conor had experienced that he was dealing with, but a system that on all accounts refused to support him. It would be another eighteen months before he asked for help again.

After years of "surviving after surviving," Conor looked for something – anything – that could protect him and his family. Both he and his mum learned there was something they could apply for called an "intervention order" – "a piece of paper, so we could feel safe" – so he called every lawyer in Mildura but "they were all conflicted out." When he couldn't find a lawyer to help them, he resorted to writing to local MPs and even federal ministers. "I'm sitting there writing these poetic letters – *We're at risk, we're unsafe, we're scared, someone help us!* I just needed someone to be like, *Mate, it's okay, I'll do this with you. This violence is not and was never your fault*. But no one ever did.

"This is the generation governments are expecting to break cycles of violence," says Conor. "But how can we be expected to break the cycle alone?"

*

Right now, hundreds of thousands of children and young people are facing the challenge of breaking the cycle of violence, and many are doing that alone. Of the almost 40,000 children and young people who showed up at specialist homelessness services in 2024, around a third were recorded as victim-survivors of family violence. Local services say that is a vast underestimate, because in their data the figure is much higher – 90 per cent of young people seeking help from Youth Off The Streets (in Sydney's inner west) grew up with family violence. Tonight, for every young person who sleeps in a refuge bed, another will be turned away.

One of the few dedicated family violence services in Australia for young unaccompanied victim-survivors of all genders is a small pilot program in Melbourne's CBD called Amplify, which operates within Melbourne's Frontyard Youth Services. It has temporary funding to help dozens of young people per year. When you rock up to Frontyard, it's hard to ignore the establishment emblazoned with gilt lettering directly opposite: the Private Eyes Gentlemen's Club. The contrast in the front windows of Frontyard is stark: bright flags and posters warmly greet young people who are First Nations and LGBTIQA+. Even the interior design – soft furnishings, wood panelling, indoor plants – is a welcome change from the hard-edged, clinical environments that usually meet young people in crisis.

Shorna Moore meets me at the front desk. Her passion and drive derive from her own experience growing up with family violence. Now, as the head of policy and advocacy for Melbourne City Mission (which runs Frontyard), she devotes her working life to helping others get the help she couldn't. Frontyard is Victoria's central access point for young people whose homes are no longer safe to live in. Kids as young as twelve come in their thousands every year; a quarter have travelled hundreds of kilometres. "They come in and use the facilities here, because they've been living on the streets and they haven't slept," says Shorna. "A lot of kids just come and eat, have a shower and wash their clothes."

Downstairs, peer workers spend their days helping young people any way they can: building social connections by hosting laser-tag games in the rumpus room, helping children's hospital staff test and immunise for STIs, and organising hospital admissions for the many young people in severe mental distress. "We've had a lot more young people die lately. Suicide is just skyrocketing, and we've done a lot of research around the link between growing up with family violence and youth suicide – like, it's huge." Every four days across Australia, a young homeless person is suiciding. "And our stats show that four out of five have experienced family violence growing up."

The Amplify pilot program occupies a small corner of the Frontyard office. Here, three specialist family violence caseworkers and a young peer support worker spend their days helping young people aged fifteen to nineteen who have been though high-risk family violence or intimate-partner violence and either can't live at home anymore or are at risk of becoming homeless. They fall outside the net of Child Protection – fifteen is usually considered too old. What staff hear is incredibly distressing: these young people are often subjected to the same kind of violence suffered by adults. There's also soul-crushing emotional abuse, "but it can take them time to recognise that as violence." In the immediate term, Amplify helps these young people make plans to help protect them, either on the street (where they may also face violence from police) or at home. To kids living with high-risk family violence, there are questions like: *Are there locks on the doors? Is there a window you can get out of? Do you have any ID? Do you have money?*

They need the kind of help they can't get anywhere else: words to understand what they've experienced, assistance to help them return to or stay in school, help dealing with police, and a hand to hold as they navigate intimidating applications for everything from income support to housing to getting an intervention order. For each young person, the Amplify team is funded to devote 140 hours (four months). But nothing happens quickly – especially in bureaucracies – so this work often takes much longer.

The pipeline from family violence to intimate-partner violence is remarkably common, affecting up to 60 per cent of Amplify's clients. "Sometimes they know they shouldn't be with them, but they need shelter, so they stay," says Moore. This is a pathway trodden by young survivors of family violence across Australia, especially those who have fled their homes. A recent Anglicare report, *Young, In Love and In Danger*, interviewed seventeen young Tasmanians who experienced intimate-partner violence in their teens. This kind of research is rare, but not as scarce as the actual services for teenage intimate-partner violence: those are "almost non-existent." As the young people explain, they dredged up the worst things that ever happened to them because they want policymakers to wake up to how bad it is and do something about it.

Jamie was fourteen and homeless the first time her boyfriend, Braden, sixteen, sexually assaulted her. "I've tried to physically fight. I ended up just getting thrown across the room into a cupboard. I just lay on the floor there crying until he fell asleep again, and then climbed into bed. At this stage I didn't have anywhere else to go, so just accepted that that happened and hoped it wouldn't happen again, but obviously it just got worse throughout the years."

The report also interviewed twenty youth workers. Most of the young women they worked with had gone from experiencing violence at home to getting together with a violent partner. Not only was the rate of gendered violence high for teenagers, it also seemed to be getting more severe. "The level of strangulation is high, the level of serious assaults is high … the verbal abuse via text sometimes is just absolutely jaw-dropping," said Jo. "I would say just anecdotally, young women are probably in more physically violent relationships than older women … and that is somewhat surprising given … young people are supposed to be getting all of this preventative stuff … But these young guys can be very traditional in their views of women and expect their girlfriends to be very submissive."

Personally, I've lost count of the number of young women I've spoken to who met their violent partner in their teens and ended up having children to them. For so many, pregnancy and childbirth accelerated the violence – and by then the chance for them to get free had slipped through their fingers. It's a no-brainer for governments to prioritise help for young people in violent relationships – not just by giving them education but by providing tangible, practical help. The urgency of this is clear in the statistics: an astonishing 28 per cent of men aged eighteen to thirty report using at least one form of physical or sexual violence against a partner.

In this area, the Amplify team has had huge success: 97 per cent of the young men, women and non-binary people they've worked with either left a violent partner or stopped using violence themselves, and they've stayed safe in the two years since. "You've got to get to it early. If you leave a whole lot of young people without help, they just grow up and enter the adult family violence system," says Moore. "Why would we wait until they're adults to provide them with a response? If we just keep ignoring this, I don't know how we're going to reduce violence."

INTERRUPTING TRANSMISSION

Violence can be transmitted from one generation to the next, and unless we address intergenerational trauma in children we are never going to make any real progress. It's not just that young people will simply grow up to repeat what they saw – what's often shorthanded as "monkey see, monkey do." Growing up in an environment of abuse attunes a young person's entire system to threat and risk. Unless someone helps them overturn that, it will be their prism for interpreting the world and their later relationships. "They grow up in a body that is expecting violence and betrayal," says Michael Salter. "That gets encoded in early childhood. And if we are unable to protect a young boy from exposure to violence, abuse and neglect, our capacity to re-regulate him later on is really limited." Of course, many of these boys grow into men who lead largely fulfilling lives. For others, that struggle to self-regulate will translate into violence. Others yet may end up being revictimised, or struggling mightily in other areas of their lives.

Until 2023, the sheer scale of childhood maltreatment in Australia could only be guessed at. We had no idea how many children were maltreated, what type of maltreatment they experienced and who did it to them, let alone how that affected them as they grew up. "Until we knew that, we didn't have a hope in hell of developing evidence-based prevention programs and policy responses," says QUT professor Ben Mathews. "So I decided to try and do a prevalence study." Mathews has spent much of his professional career trying to protect victims of child sexual abuse, driving changes to the statute of limitations as well as mandatory reporting of sexual abuse. "But the biggest problem of all," he says, "was how do we prevent this from happening in the first place?"

That idea for a prevalence study became the 2022 Australian Child Maltreatment Study: a survey of 8500 Australians, including 3500 young people aged sixteen to twenty-four, asked about their experiences before the age of eighteen. It involved questions about five types of maltreatment: physical, emotional and sexual abuse, neglect, and exposure to family and domestic violence. The results were bracing, proving once and for all that, in Australia, child maltreatment is not the exception – it's the norm. Almost two-thirds of Australians have experienced at least one form of maltreatment, and one in four have been subjected to at least three forms. For many, the impacts have been lifelong: almost half of Australians maltreated as children developed a clinical mental health disorder, compared to 21.6 per cent of people who weren't. Sexual abuse and emotional abuse were particularly harmful.

Faced with astonishing figures like these, we often reach for denial – "Surely that's not right: how do they even define 'maltreatment'?" Mathews was alive to this – "If you define things too liberally, your estimates will be too high" – which is why he spent years scouring global evidence on best-practice surveys and definitions to design the most accurate tool for measurement. He didn't want to measure a respondent's subjectivity: the question "Have you experienced sexual violence?" could be interpreted very differently by a sixty-year-old, for example, than it might be by a sixteen-year-old. So the survey asked about specific behaviours. Two questions for physical abuse, for example, measured acts of physical force (excluding lawful corporal punishment) by a parent/caregiver (including those within institutions, like teachers). Had respondents been a) hit, punched, kicked or physically hurt; or b) beaten up, hit on the head or face, choked or burnt?

Mathews and his team expected that the youngest cohort would have experienced lower rates of abuse than their parents and grandparents. But the results for young people aged sixteen to twenty-four were shocking. Compared to older Australians, the rate of exposure to domestic violence remained virtually unchanged (four in ten): sexual abuse overall was *almost* unchanged (one in four), as was neglect (one in ten), while emotional abuse had increased (to one in three). Self-harm among this cohort was also "a national crisis," affecting three in ten overall, and twice as many females (39.5 per cent) as males (20 per cent); sexual abuse and emotional abuse were strongly associated with this outcome. Of the five main maltreatment categories, only physical violence from an adult caregiver had substantially declined (to almost three in ten).

Separately, the ACMS also measured "lawful corporal punishment." Hitting, smacking and pinching your own child is legally permissible in every Australian state and territory (if done "reasonably" for the purpose of discipline), as is washing their mouth out with soap. The survey showed that, even today, more than 60 per cent of young people have been physically punished by an adult caregiver at least four times. For a country committed to ending violence in a single generation, permitting state-sanctioned violence against children is a bizarre own goal, not least because studies link physical discipline in childhood with a higher risk of committing intimate-partner violence as an adult. Corporal punishment is illegal now in sixty-five countries, including New Zealand. Australia forbids this kind of violence against other adults and pets, but for children our laws have remained unchanged since colonisation – when this practice was first introduced.

The study did show some promising progress: institutional child sexual abuse was radically reduced: compared to the rate of 2.8 per cent for Australians aged over forty-five, it was just 0.5 per cent for Australians aged sixteen to twenty-four. Also, sexual abuse by an adult family member had "pretty much halved in a generation," from 8.7 per cent down to 4.4. "When you consider that this behaviour has occurred for hundreds of years, these are just stupendous breakthroughs. It shows that huge change can happen." Young Australians were still, however, experiencing high rates of sexual abuse – it's just that their perpetrator was now more likely to be another child than an adult.

The rise of sexual abuse by other adolescents was one of the survey's most alarming findings. The other was the increase in emotional abuse, especially parental hostility and rejection. For this young cohort, emotional abuse also appeared to be more distinctly gendered – affecting 40 per cent of young women and girls and 27 per cent of young men and boys. Older-age cohorts lacked such a clear gender disparity, indicating that "in contemporary Australia, there is substantially more emotional abuse of girls than there has been in the past," says Mathews. "And it's hard to know exactly why."

The term "emotional abuse" is, for many people, highly suspect. In this age of acute sensitivity, such terms have been neutered by eyerolls and barbed dismissals: this is considered "snowflake" territory. So we need to be clear about how exactly emotional abuse was measured. Based on a rigorous review of the scientific literature, and after extensive testing and review, the ACMS asked respondents three questions, and only counted the experience as emotional abuse if the behaviour was repeated over weeks, months or years: "Did any of your parents insult you, humiliate you, or call you hurtful names?" "Did any of your parents often ignore you, or not show you love and affection?" and "Did any of your parents tell you they hated you, didn't love you, wished you were dead or had never been born?" For Mathews, the third question on rejection yielded one of the most chilling findings of the entire study. "Almost 9 per cent of Australians had that experience in childhood," he says. "Three quarters of people who experienced this said they were told that repeatedly over *years* … Emotional abuse is a type of rejection that goes to the child's core," says Mathews. "It has the capacity to annihilate the child's sense of self-worth and safety. That is a profoundly terrifying experience for a kid, because their parent is their source of safety. If that is removed, they are alone and isolated, with no sense of safety – in fact, they are under threat." The ACMS also showed that adults who had been subjected to emotional abuse in childhood suffered similar long-term harms – more mental and physical illness, more substance abuse – to those subjected to sexual abuse.

Listening to Mathews speak, I thought back to all the adult victim-survivors of coercive control who have said, over and over, that the physical violence – if they even experienced that – wasn't the worse part. For them, the worst part was the humiliation, the degradation, the feeling they were always walking on eggshells and that they had lost their sense of self. In the letter Jack wrote to his father, he said the same – though his father's physical violence was extreme, the emotional abuse was "by far the worst." It struck me with renewed force that children who are emotionally abused – whether in the context of family violence or not – may be having a parallel experience to adult victims of coercive control. Only the impact is even worse, because their feelings of self-worth and safety are being "annihilated" before they've even had a chance to properly form.

Getting a grip on emotional abuse – and directing resources to prevent it – must be a key part of our strategy to prevent gendered violence. As we'll see, the deep shame that can take over emotionally abused kids is a major risk factor for both later victimisation and perpetration. The mental health world has long understood that these experiences form shame-based parts of a person's self that are very difficult to reach through cognition, which makes those parts very difficult to treat.

For Celina, it has been heartbreaking to see the destructive impact of emotional abuse on her two younger brothers. "One of my brothers has become an abuser and is now in hospital completing a 28-day rehab program. The other is a successful programmer but lives his life almost entirely online – he's extremely preoccupied with safety."

When I first started communicating online with Celina, she struck me as intelligent, self-effacing and driven. She was intent on representing an experience that sits outside the dominant narrative on gendered violence. In Celina's family, it was her mother who was abusive – towards her father and all three children. "My mum is white, and my dad is South Asian. Mum came from a really patriarchal family – her dad was quite domineering and a serial cheater – and there was a lot of conflict between her parents." Celina remembers her mother as "super driven, glamorous and charismatic. She told the best stories at parties and was always taking us kids on adventures. She had a lot of capacity for joy, but also a huge amount of rage." Her mother was particularly fixated on the fact that Celina's father had cheated on her briefly before Celina was born. "Even when I was a kid, she would say, 'He cheated, so he deserves to be punished.' And I thought, 'Okay, that's fair enough.' You know, I was a kid – she was my sun and my moon."

As her mum's mental health declined, the violence and coercive control worsened – she monitored her husband, isolated him from his friends and shamed his Muslim faith as "disgusting." Dad often took contracts overseas "to get away from her," leaving Celina at home with her mother. From age four, Celina was left home alone for hours at a time. When her mother flew into rages, she'd beat Celina so badly she had to make up stories to explain the bruises to friends.

Celina was in high school when her two younger brothers were born. Looking after two young ones, her mother became less physically violent, but more verbally abusive around her kids. "A lot of it was about men being bad and Muslims being dirty." After Celina's dad left for another woman when her brothers were six and four, "her verbal abuse became a lot more extreme, and she developed delusions." Around her brothers, she would go into "monologues about how terrible men were and smack them violently." She was convinced that everything her children did had a sexual subtext. The paranoid delusions became extreme: "men" had placed satellites on the house to surveil and conduct experiments on her. "She was in so much mental pain, and she wasn't able to step outside it."

In her teens, Celina could escape the house to stay with supportive friends, but her much younger brothers couldn't. She reported her mum to Child Protection a few times, "but no one was interested. They told me, 'We have kids who don't have anything to eat.' There was no help." By then, her mother would rant abusively at her brothers. "It was like a freak show – her voice would range between extremely childish to this weird, rageful, serrated tone." Celina moved out, but continued doing whatever she could to help her brothers – they moved in with her when they were teenagers, and had a great relationship.

But by the time her youngest brother, Adam, was sixteen, he started getting reactive and increasingly verbally abusive. "We just thought, if we can get him into the school counsellor, and just pay lots of attention to him, maybe we can love it out of him … I didn't realise how serious it was." Later, when Adam got into his first relationships, Celina learnt that he had hit his girlfriends and was spiralling into addiction and chronic infidelity. Eventually, Celina had to pull one girlfriend aside and tell her that he wasn't safe to be around. "We were really worried about her. It's just so devastating to see someone you've always thought of as a vulnerable person start to hurt someone else in such horrendous ways." As we speak, Celina's brother is in a clinic, detoxing from prescription benzos. He's also enrolled in a men's behaviour-change program. "Rehab is the only place he's been treated for his childhood trauma."

Celina says she's relieved to hear people paying more attention to emotional abuse. "The boys had this sexualised verbal abuse directed at them, sometimes for hours a day. And still I found myself thinking, *Well, what happened to them wasn't as bad as what happened to me, because it wasn't so physically violent*. But actually in many ways it was worse, because the words were really directed at an intrinsic part of who they were." Despite the violence she endured, Celina was not the focus of the worst years of her mum's emotional abuse.

When we look at abuse from the child's point of view, the gendered violence narrative gets more complicated. Child abuse is more commonly perpetrated by men, but it's not so distinctly gendered. That's why some children of abusive mothers can find the discourse on gender-based violence deeply alienating. "I'm just so scared that no one will ever care about kids abused by their mums," says Celina. "Even as a female victim, I've started to feel like I don't matter, simply because I had the wrong perpetrator. How does that affect boys and men who have the same background as me – boys like my brothers – who are being told, *You need to change your attitude?* And how does this approach feed into things like backlash? Because I'm a feminist, and I feel actual rage about it."

*

Aside from a psychopathic minority who act with a pure instrumentality, the bravado of many perpetrators masks an insatiable hunger for intimacy and belonging, and a savage and dangerous insecurity. Over time, the innate need for love and approval they were born with has been mutated by an overpowering emotion: shame.

I've written and lectured for years on this tragic and dangerous "maladaptation," particularly the phenomenon of "humiliated fury": a cocktail of shame, rage and entitlement that gives abusive people, particularly men, a way to protect themselves against feeling powerless and defective. Other theorists call this "narcissistic rage" – a phenomenon many victim-survivors know all too much about. By blaming others, and abusing and oppressing them, these men regain a sense of power and protect themselves from what feels like looming annihilation. Indeed, the prison psychiatrist James Gilligan believes that all violence is, at its root, driven by shame. Not guilt, mind you – guilt tends to inhibit bad behaviour, whereas shame drives it. Studies demonstrate that men with elevated levels of shame (and shame-fuelled anger) are more likely to perpetrate abuse against women. The conversion of deeply buried shame into rage and violence is not inevitable. As Gilligan outlines, it's a bomb that goes off when the following factors collide: the man experiences shame as intense and overwhelming; he lacks non-violent alternatives to restore a positive sense of himself; he doesn't have the capacity for genuine remorse; and he is socialised into male gender roles that emphasise violence (or status/control) and rigid masculinity. It's not inevitable, and it's not an excuse. Many men who feel shame or jealousy don't become violent. Consider the men who, after suffering childhoods of abuse, shame or neglect, grow up vowing never to use violence themselves – and who become cycle-breakers for their own children. Or those who spend years attending to their deeply concealed shame and anger so they won't take it out on others. Men who translate shame into violence take the path of least resistance. Women and children (as well as other men) suffer horrific abuse – and sometimes death – at the hands of men who refuse to deal with the true source of their own pain and frustration.

Journalist Jane Gilmore, who has worked and reported on gender-based violence for fifteen years, has written about the connection between shame and violence: "If a man believes his masculinity is the defining characteristic of his identity, and he also believes that masculinity earns respect by being sexually dominant and aggressive, he will feel every failure to meet that standard as overwhelming shame, as evidence that he is unlovable and unworthy. The slightest hint of disrespect from others will feel to him like proof they have seen his shameful self, and they are disgusted by him. Violence, particularly sexual violence, is his means of proving to himself that he is powerful – shame*less* rather than shameful."

Practitioners I've interviewed over the years have frequently highlighted the corrosive influence of shame. Maggie Woodhead spent much of her career around the most hardcore domestic violence offenders in prisons in Western Australia. Speaking to me for *The Trap*, Woodhead said the destructive impact of shame was the key to decoding these offenders' counterintuitive accounts of their behaviour. The vast majority – 86 per cent – had grown up with family violence as children. They told her that when they were at their most violent, they felt the *opposite* of how they looked. "He's experiencing himself as smaller, more afraid, more vulnerable, more desperate, more fearful of abandonment," she told me. "He's shrinking down internally, which is why he's making himself bigger and bigger and bigger externally, until he becomes this raging monster." For Woodhead, it was clear that those deeply buried feelings of fear, shame and vulnerability that were generated in childhood were key to these men's hunger for power and control. "They are unable to self-soothe, they have very low self-worth, and they need a container for their overwhelming emotions."

That sense deep down that they are defective – that they are unlovable – is often locked away behind a firewall of grandiosity and narcissism. As the American family therapist Terry Real explained to me for *The Trap*: "Shame leads to violence in masculinity. It is a millennia-old neuron track that's inherited over generation after generation that you can transliterate shame into grandiosity. You can move from impotence to power *over*. And what's devilish about grandiosity is it feels good. It works. It pulls you out of your helplessness and you feel pumped. It's like cocaine. Cocaine is a drug that is a portal into grandiosity, and you feel big and strong and invincible … It works, but it creates havoc in your world.

"One of the few characteristics that distinguish a cohort of abusers from normal men is increased sensitivity to abandonment," Real adds. "These abusers are love addicts – grandiose love addicts. They're dependent on the warm regard of their partners. When their partners withdraw or don't give them that regard, or get mad at them, they go into a self-esteem crash. They have about two seconds' worth of tolerance for that. And then they pump up the grandiosity and they go after them. All the while feeling like they're the real victims."

As a society, we've long agreed on a narrative about abusive men: that they do it for power and control, they do it because they can, because of male privilege, because they're entitled. But a two-dimensional framing of abusive men as powerful and privileged fails to recognise that they too have a complex inner world. We remain blind to what bell hooks called "the deep inner misery of men … the terrible terror that gnaws at the soul when one cannot love."

After all, every man was once a little boy who wanted to love and be loved.

*

Jack, whom we met at the beginning of this essay, was that little boy. He desperately craved love and guidance from his father and got nothing in return but violence and degradation.

Jack was ten when he managed to escape his father one night with his mother and siblings. The readjustment to life outside the violence was surreal. "It's otherworldly," says Jack, now twenty. "You're so used to feeling like you'll never get out." But leaving his father's physical proximity was just the beginning. For Jack, his younger brother Darcy and his older sister Ruby, coercive control was the atmosphere they had lived and breathed from birth. Their father was not someone they could just leave. His anger, his sadism, his rules, his contempt – all of it was *inside* them, twisting through their nervous systems like an invasive weed. "I had all these questions, and this unfiltered anger and rage," says Jack. "You're angry at this invisible object, but you can't lash out at *him*." Ruby, also subjected to "horrific abuse," had aligned closely with their father for safety in the year before they left. After they left, Ruby emulated his "toxic traits" – especially his psychological violence – and deployed them against her mother and brothers.

Jack expected that escaping his father would give them "some space and time to heal." But like so many women and kids who flee coercive control, the family was now entering a new era of violence – post-separation control. Jack's father was arrested on a string of charges, including several counts of physical and sexual assault, stalking and intimidating, threats to kill, reckless wounding and using an offensive weapon to commit sexual assault. Theresa had collated a huge amount of evidence over the years – so much the police told her they couldn't charge him for everything. One day, shortly after Theresa returned home from court, she was "shocked" to see her ex-husband's criminal lawyers standing on their doorstep. They had followed her from court back to their safehouse. "No one should have known where we lived. We had AVOs and everything." When Theresa answered the door, the lawyers handed her papers for Family Court. It was just four months since he'd been arrested, and now, with his criminal case in train, *his* parents were applying for full custody of the children. "They were claiming I was abusive, that I didn't cook good meals for the children – the list was huge."

In an effort to destroy Theresa's relationship with her children, Mark's parents reported her to Child Protection for failing to get the kids to school. The kids *had* stopped going to school – they were prohibited from returning because the teachers were so intimidated by the threats their father had sent. When Child Protection came to investigate, Theresa was threatened with child removal and mandated to do a parenting program. They enforced another condition: that Theresa write a letter of apology to her children. Jack's voice shakes as he remembers this. "It was shattering, because here was the one person in our life who actually *wanted* to save us and did everything in her power to do that – and now she was *apologising* to us." The other condition – that she also write an apology to her ex-husband – Theresa refused. Eventually, with the support of her domestic-violence caseworkers, "it all came to a head." "Child Protection ended up having to apologise to me," Theresa says, "because they realised, 'Oh, it's coercive control.' The whole thing had been a big lie. I wasn't abusive, and I hadn't done anything wrong. It was a really, really terrible situation."

There was no space, no safety – no freedom. "There was this constant threat looming over us that anything could change and you could go back to *him* or to *them* [his father's parents]," says Jack. "It was so heavy, and it didn't give me a single chance to heal. It didn't give me time to understand and sort of place these feelings I was having and what I was going through. It made things very stressful and very angry. I wanted that space. I wanted to be left alone." In this state of chaos, Jack started inflicting violence on Theresa. "I was following in the footsteps of my father and using all these behaviours – like name-calling, outward aggression and physical violence towards Mum – that I desperately needed to unlearn." Jack, then just eleven years old, urgently needed reassurance that his family was safe, to be helped by someone with the skills to unpack his trauma and self-blame, and given techniques to help him manage his explosive anger. "It was such a split-second sort of reaction I'd learnt off him – straight to anger, nought to a hundred. No thinking – just violence." Desperate to find help for her children, Theresa had to become their full-time caseworker, going to endless "meetings, meetings, meetings" – mostly in vain. Says Jack, "The support I got was basically nil compared to what I needed."

Eleven-year-old Jack became suicidal, and when his violence became untenable Theresa had to make the heartbreaking decision to call the police. "I understand now how hard that must have been for Mum," says Jack, "but having that confrontation with police was very scary, and very hard: it put me in this place where I felt like I *was* him, and I felt like I couldn't escape this fate." Jack was committed to a mental health ward, where he was put on an experimental cocktail of medication. "It felt like these people who were meant to be protecting and helping me were just taking me away."

Speaking to Jack now, you'd never guess what he's been through. His tone is mature and respectful, and he has obvious deep affection and respect for his mother. Theresa spent years of her life helping Jack and his siblings recover. "I have had to use my super and savings to survive. I was my children's psychologist, nurse, teacher, role model, therapist and ambulance," she says.

After years of psychological assessments and Family Court dates, Theresa was finally granted full custody. Retaining care of her own children cost

Theresa hundreds of thousands of dollars in legal fees. Once the threats of Family Court and Child Protection had passed, Theresa could finally bring routine back into their lives. She names this as the key to her success. "After trying to implement so many positive strategies, the best thing for my children was to have a safe routine and provide predictability back into our lives."

Jack spent years deconstructing the toxic beliefs imparted by his father. Eventually, he was able to interrupt those split-second violent responses – to take a breath in those reactive moments and put words to how he was feeling. "Every time someone would say something to me, at first, I'd be like, 'That's easier said than done – you haven't lived my life.' But eventually, through reinforcement and positive female role models like Mum, I was able to start really hearing it, and the repetition eventually started to kick in."

No interventions, however, have been enough for Ruby, now twenty-three. Before her father was granted parole, she was "doing remarkably well" and had started a degree in nursing. In the two years since his release, she has barely left the house. She is addicted to laxatives and self-harms compulsively. Her organs are struggling, especially her heart, and she still cannot talk about the violence she endured. In January, mental health discharged her from care. "She is too complex," says Theresa.

Jack still struggles with the effects of complex trauma, but he is optimistic about the future and has just enrolled to study counselling. He is living proof that the right intervention at the right time can turn a life around. For so many other families, however, there is no intervention – and ultimately, it's not just these men's future girlfriends and wives that pay the price, but also their mothers.

*

Older women are hardly seen in media reports on domestic homicide, yet they are being killed in record numbers: in 2017, 2018 and 2023, women over fifty-five were killed at a rate *double* the national average. In 2024, eight women were allegedly murdered by their sons. "When we talk about violence against women, it's always a younger woman fleeing with two little kids hanging around her knees," said Yumi Lee, from the Older Women's Network. "You rarely see any commentary about all the women who grow old with violence, who live with, maybe, sons who are violent. They are really invisible." Catherine Barrett, director of Celebrate Ageing, says older Australian mothers are facing a "perfect storm": the twin crises of mental health and cost-of-living, which are pushing a growing number of recently separated violent men to move back in with their parents. "The mothers are not reporting their sons," Barrett told *Guardian Australia*, "because this is their son, and it's shame on the family, and they're worried about his mental health."

"It's also shameful, though, right? For mothers with violent sons, there's a feeling they have to protect them, even if they're just a horror in their lives," says 25-year-old Riannah. She is a straight-talking young woman who has already achieved enormous career success – in her day job she oversees a multi-million-dollar grant-making portfolio, backing early-stage innovators working on the most pressing social problems. "I care very deeply about a lot of things." She speaks to me because she knows most mothers with violent sons – including her own – feel they can't. Since before she can remember, she has had to watch her older brother Bill perpetrate violence against her mother. "He's so abusive – he will call her nonstop, threaten to kill himself, threaten to self-harm, steal, whatever – just to get money from her. Mum is sixty-four and has taken on additional work, just to give him money. She's given him, like, $30,000 over the course of a year. All of that went on ice dealers, gambling, whatever else."

Riannah loves her mother and says she can talk to her about anything. "She is very wise. It's not her fault that Bill is the way that he is. But he's not the little boy that she loved and looked after. He is an abuser." Bill is thirty-five now, and in and out of jail. Several family members have had to get intervention orders against him, as have two of his former partners. Riannah says the intimate-partner violence was life-threatening, including violent strangling. The likelihood that Bill will take responsibility for his actions is severely undermined by multiple addictions, as well as severe mental health problems. "He's been put into hospital a few times on involuntary treatment orders for psychosis. He believes there's a chip in his brain and people are watching him … His story is just supremely sad, in the sense that he had these experiences as a child."

Bill was only a few years old when his mother packed up him and his two siblings in the middle of the night and fled from his violent father. While they were hiding in a women's refuge, Bill's mother met the man who would become Riannah's father. Eventually, the Family Court granted her sole custody of Bill and his siblings. Now partnered with Riannah's father, his mother was seeking a fresh start and moved from New South Wales to Queensland. But moving interstate annulled the Family Court orders, and Bill's father took his mother back to court. This time, a different judge decided the violence wasn't such a huge risk and ordered Bill to stay with his father during school holidays. He was visiting him for the first time when Riannah was born. That one visit was a disaster that would plague him for the rest of his life. "His father introduced him to drugs, beat him up, and left him at an orphanage."

Riannah would grow up in the shadow of her brother's violence. She doesn't have many memories from childhood, "but some of the memories I do have are of my brother smashing down the windows, throwing plates around. He struggled with various addictions." The violence continued into Riannah's teens, by which time her brother was in his twenties. She does vividly remember being with her friends at high school and discovering the interactive Queensland Crime Map. "It showed crime hotspots that had the most police call-outs – basically, which neighbours you should avoid." When Riannah's friends urged her to put in her address, the results were "humiliating." "It was like, 'Red alert – do not go to this house.'"

"Mum managed to escape a violent partner who almost killed her. But now she's in another domestic violence relationship with her son. For forty years now she's been living with abuse," says Riannah, who sees only two likely solutions: "Either she dies or he does … It's taken me a long time to come to that realisation, but I really believe that's true."

On several measures, Riannah is a major success story: she has emerged from a violent childhood to lead a brilliant, satisfying life: "I love my job, I love my friends, I love my family. I have possibly, like, the best relationship on earth." But she knows she didn't come away from her brother's violence unscathed. That childhood had to be adapted to somehow, and Riannah's adaptation was to develop a more "avoidant" attachment style: very successful and driven, with an intense need for independence, difficulty feeling the full extent of her emotions and a fear of having children of her own. "I used to think I was just indifferent, but I'm actually deeply scared."

*

All over Australia, single parents – mostly mothers – are scrambling to find something, anything, to help their children recover and prevent them repeating the cycle of violence. These single mothers – almost entirely unsupported – are Australia's unofficial reserve army of prevention agents. I meet them at community halls in every state and territory, in cities and in country towns. Their questions are always the same: *Where can I find help for my children? Nobody will help!* What these mothers know instinctively is that a teenager who is violent to their family members and intimate partners is much more likely to use violence as an adult. That's also clear in the data, says Hayley Boxall, and yet there's "maybe a handful of services" targeted specifically at adolescents using violence. "I just don't understand why we're not doing more with these kids. During adolescence, we've got way more levers to get them engaged in services. We can leverage parents. We can leverage education systems. This is all low-hanging fruit, and it's just so crucial for disrupting the intergenerational transmission of violence. We're completely missing the boat on it."

"Recovery and Healing" is now a priority area in the Second National Plan. It's one of few things that sets the Second Plan apart from the First. As we've seen, recovery and healing for victim-survivors isn't just a nice thing to have; it's the key to breaking cycles of violence. Recovery *is* prevention.

For this reason, governments should invest in trauma and recovery services across Australia – that much is obvious. But no amount of money will ever be enough until governments are willing to end the violence inflicted by their own systems. For many victims, the violence has two key stages: what's done to them by the perpetrator, and then what's done to them by "the system." Much critical attention has rightly been focused on the many terrible failings of police and the courts, but in stories about family and domestic violence, other systems are less often interrogated. Three systems – family law, child protection and youth justice – are highlighted by victim-survivors time and again. At the very moment when children need care and connection, these three systems too often step in to traumatise them further.

We've seen already how child protection and family law influenced the perpetration trajectories of Jack and Bill. Stories like this are legion. While governments commit increased levels of funding to "end violence within a single generation," their own systems are loading up the pipeline of future victims and perpetrators.

These are the young people we recognise as "victims in their own right." And this is what we do to them.

*

Lily is sixteen. She can't remember her life before Family Court; the court battle to decide where she would live began when she was three, soon after her mother fled Lily's abusive father: she was ordered by the court to live five nights a fortnight with her father. Her earliest memories are of sleeping with her father's dog, sometimes outside, sometimes in the laundry. It was hard for Lily to find space to put her things: her father was a hoarder, and there were piles of rubbish on almost every available surface. At night, as Lily was trying to sleep on the lounge, she could hear rodents chewing on her belongings.

As Lily grew older, her father's need for power and control fixated on her. At mealtimes – the only time her father would spend time with her – he would serve her adult portions and if she didn't finish everything on her plate, he would punish her by locking her outside. Lily would wait in the dark, knowing that even if she wanted to run away, she couldn't – the property was surrounded by bushland, with a long driveway leading to the road. Lily knew that the neighbours wouldn't even hear her scream.

When Lily would return to her mother's house for the other nine nights in the fortnight, it would take her two days to come down from her hyper-vigilant state. "At first I would be distraught – crying and throwing things. Then I'd have a few days of happiness, hanging out with friends," she explains. "Then another three days, feeling upset about having to return to Dad. I would cry and scream, but there was nothing Mum could do – if she didn't return me to Dad, as the court had ordered her to do, we knew she might lose care of me altogether." So Lily would return to her father, who she was convinced would end up killing her.

It may shock readers to learn this, but once a parenting order is made it is virtually impossible for children to resist. If they do run away from an abusive parent, their custodial parent can apply for a recovery order and the court can then order federal police to track the child down and return them. One teenager I interviewed, "Carly," was pursued by federal police after she ran away from her father, who controlled and intimidated her and had been violent to her mother and brother. She had to threaten suicide before the police would relent. They did so only on the proviso she was taken to hospital; after she was released, she stayed for four months in a refuge. Eventually, she was allowed to return to her mother – but only because the court decided she was old enough to make her own decision.

In previous centuries, judges could order an abused woman to return to her husband. The idea of such an order seems unthinkable now – but that is exactly what the family law system still does to some children, even when kids openly disclose abuse and say unequivocally that they are terrified and do not want to see their abusive parent – even when that testimony is corroborated by other professionals, including police, social workers, teachers and doctors. Recent data collected by the Family Court shows that over 80 per cent of its caseload involves allegations of family violence. Essentially, the family law courts have become family violence courts by default.

The Albanese government has shown considerable courage in its efforts to improve the family law system's approach to child safety, especially by overturning key sections of the *Family Law Act* (like the presumption of equal shared parenting, introduced by the Howard government in 2006) which made it even harder for women and children to leave violence. They have introduced high-quality family violence training for all professionals working in the court. And yet I am still getting desperate emails from mothers who have fled violent partners and whose kids have disclosed their own abuse, only to be ordered to live with their abusive parent. It goes without saying that these cases are incredibly complex, and there are many judges who consider them with the utmost care and expertise. But there are still too many judges who don't, and too many professionals working across the system who don't understand coercive control or child development.

On this point, Hayley Boxall is emphatic: "The family law courts actively make decisions that make children less safe." Boxall is often called on to write expert reports for the court. She sees time and again how Family Court orders can undermine the recovery of children. "You've got this poor single mum who is trying to manage their child's behaviours, and the Family Court orders this young person to go and see Dad – even when there's a history of intimate-partner violence," says Boxall. "Because the court goes, *Well, just because he was violent towards you doesn't mean there's a risk for the kids* – which is just rubbish. Then, if the court orders shared parenting, any decision she tries to make for her kid – in terms of treatment, medical care, intervention – has to be approved by Dad." Boxall says that in her research with victim-survivors, she's spoken to women who have turned up to hospital with a child who is self-harming and suicidal, only to be sent home "because Dad won't sign off on them getting treatment … I know that the reforms have come through, and we'll wait with bated breath to see whether or not that's made any difference. I've just heard too many horror stories."

When Lily was thirteen, her mum was finally able to get the case heard again. This time, her father didn't bother contesting, so Lily was free to choose. She hasn't spoken to her father in the four years since. She has found it hard to readjust to her newfound safety and to life as an adolescent, because she never expected to live this long. Since returning to her mother, she has been diagnosed with complex PTSD. "I just wish someone had actually gone to see his house – they would have seen that it was not somewhere a kid should be living. Also, the court knew my older siblings had intervention orders against him. Why would you send a toddler to live alone with someone like that?"

*

For other children who have grown up with family violence or maltreatment – particularly First Nations kids – it won't be the family law system that decides who cares for them, but child protection.

The taxpayer money spent on child protection and youth detention is truly eye-watering: on average, it costs $400,000 to remove a child from their family, and $3320 per day – $1.12 million per year – to jail them. Many of these children are victim-survivors of violence and abuse: the very same kids the National Plan vows to protect. It's no secret that these systems are doing children and young people irreparable harm. And yet little changes. For the National Children's Commissioner, this kind of wilful blindness is on a par with climate change denial: "You've got the science right in front of you and choose not to believe it." Twelve years' worth of royal commissions and inquiries into child protection and youth justice have produced more than 3000 recommendations, "many of them repeated again and again and again," says Commissioner Anne Hollonds. "We're not listening, we're not believing the science, we're not doing what we need to do to fix this problem."

For too many kids removed into out-of-home care, "the next station on the train line," says Hollonds, "is the youth justice system." The throughline from child protection to youth justice is so common that they're known as "crossover kids." Victoria's Principal Commissioner for Children and Young People, Liana Buchanan, puts it bluntly: "We are criminalising child trauma." Victoria, a progressive state that prides itself on leading the nation on gendered violence, has removed the highest percentage of Aboriginal children, double the national average. If they spend at least two years in residential care, where they are supervised by paid staff, there's a fifty-fifty chance they'll be charged with an offence. In some cases, police are called for incidents as minor as breaking a plate, throwing a sponge, nicking food from the communal kitchen. Victorian Legal Aid even saw a child charged for damaging property when they were harming themselves. Kids who end up incarcerated can be kept in some of the most inhumane environments.

"I saw the conditions these children were being held in," Hollonds told a parliamentary briefing in 2023. "In some cases for twenty-two to twenty-three hours per day, locked in a cell on their own, not getting any kind of education, rehabilitation or care." Some of them had been in and out of jail since they were ten. "When I inquired about who would help them when they left the prison, it was basically nobody. They had no adult to back them and they saw no future. They really saw it as inevitable they'd end up in the adult jail."

More than a million dollars a year to lock up one child. That money is just being "thrown away," says Hollonds. "It could be used to address the underlying causes of crime."

It's not even that hard to prevent youth crime, as so many excellent programs have shown. In the early 2000s, for example, a demonstration program called Pathways to Prevention provided early support in preschool for kids and their families in several ethnically diverse, disadvantaged suburbs across Brisbane. The target area was chosen because it had a youth crime rate that was, in the 1990s, more than eight times the Brisbane average. Twenty years later there was a 50 per cent reduction in kids entering the youth justice system. The program targeted key risk factors: low academic achievement, poor parenting, child impulsivity and poverty. For the kids, specialist language teachers were brought into preschools to teach them oral language and communication, so they would be better prepared for school. As Griffith University's Dr Jacqueline Allen explained to RN *Breakfast*, language skills are critically important. "Children behind in communication skills may have conflict with peers and teachers, and they don't do as well in school. These things can kind of cascade." The kids in the Pathways program had better academic skills when they started school and were better behaved in class – for years. "It was that behavioural boost that we linked to a lower likelihood of getting involved with the youth justice system when they were adolescents." For the parents, there was practical support: help managing their children's behaviour, parent life skills training, peer support groups, individual support and counselling, help liaising with schools and government agencies. That support was critical – most of our interventions with young people put the burden to change on them, neglecting improvements in how they are being cared for.

From July 2025, the Albanese government has guaranteed it will subsidise three days per week of early childhood education for kids across Australia. With more children from disadvantaged homes in preschool, it's an obvious step to look at how programs like Pathways could be integrated, at least in areas with higher rates of youth crime. "These things all have a cost, but there's a huge saving compared with the cost of youth detention later on," says Allen. "And it has benefits beyond just the reduction in crime." That includes preventing gendered violence – because it addresses two major risk factors: hanging out with violent peers, and poor parenting.

*

Before we focus more on how governments could expand prevention *and* save money, let's go back one station down the line, to child protection.

Djirra, headed by Antoinette Braybrook, provides wrap-around support for Aboriginal women experiencing family violence, aiming to keep kids safe and together with their mums. In her public advocacy, Braybrook is fearless and firm, fighting at the micro and macro levels for the rights of First Nations women and kids. To this work she also brings enormous heart. "In Djirra's experience," she says, "the threat of child removal is frequently used as a form of coercive control by perpetrators against Aboriginal mothers." The vast majority of the Aboriginal women Djirra works with are partnered with non-Indigenous men. "[The men] do it to inject fear and stop Aboriginal women from reporting violence to police or seeking assistance from family violence support organisations. Aboriginal women often fear the system more than their abuser."

Braybrook is one of countless First Nations advocates and academics who have for decades been pushing against the brick wall of government denial. Lauded experts, including Professor Megan Davis, have written shocking and forensic reports uncovering the daily horrors women and kids experience at the hands of Child Protection. As these reports gather dust on government shelves, more and more kids are removed: today, almost 45 *per cent* of children across Australia who are living in out-of-home care are Aboriginal. In 2023, almost 20,000 Indigenous children were in out-of-home care, and they are being removed at 10.5 times the rate of non-Indigenous children. The escalation in removals is so significant it's being labelled a second Stolen Generation.

"Family violence is the single biggest driver of Aboriginal child removal," says Braybrook. "Aboriginal women are judged, punished and blamed for the violence they experience." In a case in Megan Davis's 2019 "Family Is Culture" review, an Aboriginal mother, needing help to leave her abusive partner, called caseworkers to her home. While they were there, the father physically assaulted the mother and was emotionally abusive towards her and the kids. After leaving for a while, the father returned, hurled more abuse at the mother and told caseworkers about her "excessive drinking." On the strength of his allegation, the caseworkers turned from helping the mother to making a snap decision to remove her children. The mother was aghast: "No, you aren't taking my babies, I called you for help today."

"Australians may assume that children are only removed when there is a dire and direct threat to a child's survival or wellbeing," says Braybrook, "but we see children being removed from Aboriginal mums over very minor issues." Braybrook says that Aboriginal mothers are often actively discouraged from seeking legal advice: they're told that child protection is not a legal issue and that involving lawyers will only complicate matters. She and other specialist Aboriginal organisations have long advocated for an automatic referral system, which would link Aboriginal mums with legal support at the point when Child Protection is notified. "Early referral for legal advice to specialist organisations like Djirra is critically important to keep Aboriginal kids with their mums."

Sometimes there really is no other option but to remove a child – the danger posed by their parents or carers is just too great. And in the best cases, those kids will end up with a Child Protection worker who advocates for them, and with carers who give them the kind of love they could never get from their parents. But in a shocking number of cases, it's the opposite. What's so baffling about this approach is that, so often, removal could have been prevented – and for a fraction of the cost – simply by *supporting* the family.

Natalie Siegel-Brown has worked in and around child protection for decades. Until recently, she was the managing director of Child Wise, a non-profit organisation safeguarding children all over the world, and she is a specialist adviser to the UN and the Fijian government in child protection systems. She has seen up close the devastating harm that child removal can transmit from one generation to the next. "When I was doing child death reviews, I never once – never once! – did an inquiry where the parents of the child who was killed had not been in the child protection system themselves. And, of course, family violence was a dominant feature across most of them." Siegel-Brown says it's not enough to tinker at the edges – the whole system needs to be reinvented. "Instead of a Child Protection worker going into a home and asking first, 'Should I remove this child?' what if the questioning flipped to, 'What's going on in this family? Is Mum unsafe? How do we keep Mum safe so she can keep her child safe? Do we need to remove a perpetrator? Or, in fact, is the broader issue here that they just need some support inside the house?'"

On the rare occasions that a Child Protection manager goes rogue, they have shown that an alternative is not just possible, but immediately effective. "There was one regional executive director," says Siegel-Brown, "and I'll never forget it. She was like, 'I can't upend the system, but I've got $2 million that's not tied to a program. So I'm going to take ten families where the kids are borderline removal and see if I can reverse the paradigm. I'm going to force the worker to go in and actually try to understand the cause of the family's dysfunction and work out what we can put into the home to support them.'" In one family, a severely disabled Aboriginal boy was living with his grandmother, who had dementia and was forgetting to feed and medicate him. Instead of removing him, workers arranged for a nurse to come to the house twice a day to help with cooking and medication. "They were just going to remove this kid, who'd been living with Grandma for ten years," says Siegel-Brown, "and then they get a nurse in to support Grandma and boom! No issues." Overall, at a cost of $75,000 per family (less than a quarter of the cost of removal), this manager stopped *nine out of ten* children being removed. Two years later, none had come back to the attention of the child protection system, which is extremely unusual – "normally, it's a revolving door. This is simple shit you could do, even in the existing system," says Siegel-Brown.

Children removed into out-of-home care typically end up in kinship care, with foster carers or in residential care. Some, however, will end up in what's known as "alternative care arrangements" – a benign term for a terrible stopgap which sees children moved into temporary accommodation – hotels, caravans, motels and short-term rentals – and supervised by workers contracted from labour-hire companies on eight-hour shifts. While ACAs are used across the country, the extent of it has only been revealed in New South Wales, in the landmark report from the NSW Advocate for

Children and Young People, Zoë Robinson, *Moving Cage to Cage*. The title came from the words of one young man who spent more than 500 days being moved around: "[They] just move me around like a doggy in the pound pretty much, moving cage to cage." ACAs are unbelievably expensive and can cost upwards of $2 million per child *per year*. Over six years, the use of ACAs cost the NSW government an astonishing $500 million.

"When I first worked in youth homelessness, people said to me, 'It's cheaper for us to put all of these kids into a private boarding school,'" Robinson tells me. "People say that flippantly, right? But you know, $70,000 is the most expensive boarding school in New South Wales, and for that amount they're guaranteed to have a great education and three meals a day."

Moving Cage to Cage landed like a bomb. The testimonies from kids put into ACA are damning: when eleven-year-old Lachlan James Hobman was removed from his home in 2016, he had to live in nine separate hotels and motels. It was "hell. The worst experience of my life." In one hotel, his workers forbade him from leaving his room for almost a week; in another, he found cockroaches in his bed. "I was abused as a child," he said, "but having my mental health completely break and having no hope at all, that's what did the most damage. I am haunted by my past, but the system is what truly put me down."

In her report, Robinson was clear: alternative care arrangements should not be used under any circumstances. To her credit, the NSW Minister for Families and Communities, Kate Washington, moved quickly, reducing the number of kids in these arrangements by 100 in less than a year. Washington described the system as "broken" and promised more reforms. The Minns government says it intends to ban this practice altogether. The extent of its use beyond New South Wales is unknown.

Why is a government content to support a system its own ministers describe as "broken"? "I think where government gets stuck, it's, 'Well, hang on, so you're telling us to completely up-end what we're doing?' This is not just about tweaking an existing system – we need to burn it down and redo the whole model," says Siegel-Brown. "There's this sense of risk – what if we burn it down and start again and it doesn't work? What do we do in the transition? It would take tremendous political bravery and will to do it, but I think it can be done. The system needs a new paradigm."

*

Sheryl Batchelor is a proud Aboriginal woman with ancestral ties to Kunja, and the head of the Yiliyapinya centre, which means "brain" in Wankamura (Gilai) language. Speaking to her is like being shown a brave new world – and by someone who does her work with the utmost love and dedication. Batchelor acts on the science that shows that brains wired in childhood to anticipate threat and risk can be changed – and that children's trajectories can be radically redirected for a fraction of the cost of jailing them. That's the work she does at Yiliyapinya, a not-for-profit that works intensively with Aboriginal and Torres Strait Islander children and their carers to improve their brain health and help them heal. "We see the 'worst of the worst,'" she tells me. "We've got children who are excluded from school, excluded from resi [residential] care and living on their own with child safety workers. All of our children have youth justice orders of some sort. They are in and out of detention. I want to take on the most vulnerable ones – the ones where everyone else is going, 'We don't know what else to do.'"

It was reading Norman Doidge's *The Brain that Changes Itself* that inspired Sheryl to make a late-career change from being an assistant principal in a Queensland primary school to a trained practitioner in "neuroplasticity" – in which certain experiences and routines can reorganise and rewire our brains. Training and mentoring with neuroscientists in Canada, America and Australia, Batchelor had a life-changing realisation: if children's brains can be damaged by trauma, then they can be *rewired* with certain routines and experiences. "But what was missing was our culture – our healing," she tells me. "So how can we improve the brain, heal the brain and help our kids and people flourish?"

As we speak, a young boy walks into the room holding a bag of Minties. Sheryl lights up.

“Hello, darling,” she says, “are they for me? Why am I getting a packet of Minties?” Sheryl explains that yesterday, the boy bearing Minties graduated Year 6. “That was a pretty special day!” she exclaims.

“Not when they showed my baby photos,” he says.

“Oh yeah, that would have been embarrassing, but well done! You should be very proud of yourself.”

When he leaves the room, Sheryl turns back to me and tells me that this gorgeous boy had, until recently, been self-harming to extreme levels. “He was just really crying out – ‘I’ve got something to say, and I don’t know how to say it,’” she says.

His story is terrible, and I include some details of it here only to highlight the kind of change that is possible when we make the right intervention early. I’ll call him “Luke.”

Luke’s father went to jail after almost killing Luke’s mother in front of him and his three siblings. That afforded the family some protection but left his mum unable to pay the rent. While a man was renting out a room in the family home, he raped Luke’s brother. Luke was in their shared bedroom when it happened. “He saw that and he froze.” Eventually Luke’s brother spoke up and police got involved. Meanwhile, Luke’s behaviour at home and at school was chaotic and nobody knew why. When Luke’s mum turned to alcohol and drugs to cope, nobody offered her help – instead, they removed her four kids and put them in residential care. That was where Luke tried to sexually assault his sister. “After that, they took him away from his brother and sisters, and placed him on his own with two workers,” Batchelor explains. “The others were getting counselling and support, but he refused it.” By the time Child Protection referred Luke to Sheryl, he’d been excluded from school after being violent to another student. Sheryl and her team agreed to work with him intensively – for five days a week. Little by little, Luke started opening up. “When he started sharing bits of his story with us, we learnt that he felt so much shame from not being able to stop his brother from being raped. He told us he was trying to act it out with his little sister so he could stop the rape himself. And it was going around and around in his head.”

Sheryl relies on philanthropy and a little federal funding, but recieves no meaningful funding from the state government. "All they've got for him is, 'Go and see a psychologist.' Then he would be left just spending every day in a resi care on his own with two support workers, going, 'What the fuck am I doing here?'"

It's no good only attending to Luke – to give him the best chance at healing, his mum needs help too. "So what we're doing now is bringing Mum in with her support people, and helping her learn how to help him," says Batchelor. "Because he's still very angry with her. So we teach her how to respond when he responds angrily to her. And we bring her here for the cultural activities, so she can just be around, and we can help her get reattached to him through play." On Friday nights, Yiliyapinya runs Made by Mob, which sees a child and their family member pair up with a carpenter to build a picnic table together that they can paint and take home. It's not just woodwork – it's another way to help rewire those damaged connections. "It's meant to press the frustration buttons. It's going to be hard, because Mum has to hold the wood while her son tries to cut it, and he's going to get it wrong. We're trying to get her to see, 'What's my brain doing here?' It's all about helping Mum self-regulate, and helping him self-regulate when Mum's around. But it needs us around to help co-regulate both of them together."

Batchelor is quick to point out that she prefers to focus on brain health, not trauma. "There's so much talk about trauma, which comes from this real deficit perspective. I had one of the kids say to me yesterday, 'It's my trauma, Aunty Sheryl,' and I said, 'No, it's not. Trauma doesn't define you. We're going to help you understand and rewire that. That part of your brain that's feeling hurt? You're going to stand up to that part and you're going to give it big cuddles and kisses, and you're going to say, 'I've got this.' But before we do that, we need to understand what it's trying to tell you, because it's trying to tell you something. It's not that you're too traumatised, it's that your brain is not able to deal with this – *yet*.'"

SOLVING THE PUZZLE

For millennia, humans have been seeking answers to a seemingly insoluble puzzle. Why do people commit acts of cruelty and violence? What are the root causes of destructive behaviour? Is violence a fundamental, unchangeable part of human nature? We've sought to answer these questions through religion, philosophy and science – and, more recently, through a revolutionary analysis of power known as feminism. Men's violence against women and children has been with us for millennia too, but for the first time in human history we have sought not just to manage such violence but to end it altogether.

Australia took a bold and courageous step fifteen years ago: to stop accepting such violence as inevitable. Led by some of the best evidence available at the time, we set out to change the way Australians experience, think and feel about gender and power. It was a uniquely ambitious vision, and a grand experiment. Many people have dedicated themselves to proving this hypothesis: that if a country can successfully alter its underlying social conditions, a reduction in violence will follow.

Somewhere along the way, however, this hypothesis hardened into something more like doctrine. But evidence is not static – it must be constantly evaluated and updated. When new evidence is found, we must remain curious and open to what it can teach us.

This essay does not suggest we discard the current approach. But we must update it. Prevention work has to find a way into the minds and bodies of those who are most likely to act violently – sexually, physically, emotionally – and persuade them not to do so. If our prevention strategy cannot do that, because it fails to incorporate and apply new evidence, we risk not only failing to reduce men's violence against women and children, but also losing the nation's faith that this goal is even possible. If this faith is lost, we face the very real danger of slipping back into a position of tacit surrender – an acceptance that this problem is intractable and will not be improved by any amount of money or effort.

If this essay is calling for anything, it is to unify and act on the many evidence-based approaches to this wicked problem.

No country in the world has cracked the problem of violence against women and children. With courage, Australia could be the first.

SOURCES

5 "a significant and sustained reduction": Nour Haydar, "Governments release joint strategy seeking to end violence against women and children within a generation", ABC News online, 16 October 2022.

5 almost 10,000 reports per week: My calculations, based on the latest available data from individual states and territories.

6 thirty-two times: Australian Institute of Health and Welfare, *Family, Domestic and Sexual Violence in Australia*, Cat. no. FDV 2, AIHW, Canberra, 2018.

6 seven times: Samantha Bricknell and Hannah Miles, *Homicide of Aboriginal and Torres Strait Islander Women*, Statistical Bulletin no. 46, Australian Institute of Criminology, Canberra, 2024.

6 "quite rightly", "round-the-clock national media coverage": Chay Brown and Karla Glynn Braun, "The NT's domestic violence inquest revealed unspeakable horrors. It would be hypocrisy to ignore the solutions", *Guardian Australia*, 27 November 2024.

6 "it will not replicate": Antoinette Braybrook, "The time is now for a First Nations National Safety Plan", NIT, 18 October 2021, nit.com.au/18-10-2021/2417/the-time-is-now-for-a-first-nations-national-safety-plan, accessed 10 February 2025.

7 "victim-survivors in their own right": Department of Social Services, *National Plan to End Violence Against Women and Children 2022–2032*, Commonwealth of Australia, 2022, p. 45.

8 "prevalence of violence": Department of Social Services, National Plan Outcomes Framework: Performance Management Plan, Commonwealth of Australia, 2024, p. 10.

9 a 28 per cent rise: This sudden escalation interrupted a thirty-year downward trend, in which time all types of homicide became less common.

9–10 number of women who had their movements tracked: Anne Summers, "How tech became the next frontier in domestic violence", *The Saturday Paper*, 16 March 2024.

10 "No government": Kate Ellis, Joint media release with Attorney-General Robert McClelland, 15 February 2011.

10 "We are all responsible": Darren Hine in "How do we tackle domestic violence" Here's what seven police chiefs had to say", *Guardian Australia*, 2 November 2014.

12 "Violence against women is not inevitable": Anastasia Powell, "Change the story: how the world's first national framework can help prevent violence against women", *The Conversation*, 13 November 2015.

13 "The elephant in the room": Mary Barry, "Prevention of violence against women – finally, an idea whose time has come", *Guardian Australia*, 20 April 2016.

13 "We have nothing": Lara Fergus in Gay Alcorn, "Australians are being told that gender inequality is the root cause of domestic violence. But is it?", *Guardian Australia*, 19 February 2016.

13 other best-practice prevention frameworks: In the framework used by the Violence Prevention Alliance, for instance, a constellation of risk factors are listed. See: who.int/groups/violence-prevention-alliance/approach. This is also reflected in Prevention Collaborative's 'Risk Factors for Intimate Partner Violence'. See: prevention-collaborative.org/wp-content/uploads/2021/08/Prevention-Collaborative_2020_Understanding-Causes-of-VAW.pdf.

14 four "gendered drivers": After pressure from Aboriginal academics and advocates, *Change the Story* was revised in 2021 to acknowledge that gendered drivers are "influenced" by other systemic and structural forms of social injustice, discrimination and oppression, including racism, ableism, ageism, heteronormativity, cissexism, class discrimination, and – for Aboriginal and Torres Strait Islander women – the contemporary impacts of colonialism. In this second version, it is also acknowledged that gender inequality and gendered drivers "may not be the most significant factor in every context." Nevertheless, the gendered drivers are still the most heavily focused on in practice.

14 addressing the gendered drivers: While *Change the Story* recommended some attention be paid to the reinforcing factors, in practice, they were largely sidelined, to the point of becoming almost invisible.

14 "an explosion" and "'This is a story'": Alcorn, "Australians are being told".

15 "all people": Our Watch, *Putting the Prevention of Violence Against Women into Practice: How to change the story*, Melbourne, 2017, p. 34.

16 "It was put strongly" and "In my view": Marcia Neave, 20th Annual New Zealand Law Foundation Ethel Benjamin Commemorative Address, Dunedin, 14 July 2016.

16 Neave was relieved: Ultimately, however the Victoria Royal Commission recommendations favoured the gender equality camp.

17 "Of course it's a hypothesis": Partridge in Alcorn, "Australians are being told".

17 "We do know": Patty Kinnersly on *The Project*, 22 May 2019.

19 "inspirational work ethic": Euan Black, "How 'toxic masculinity' attacks pushed boys to Andrew Tate", *Australian Financial Review*, 27 December 2024

19 "forging tribes", "Solitude and the rise of singles", etc.: Alice Evans, "The Great Splintering: how digital tech shattered cultural control", *The Great Gender Divergence*, 28 January 2025, ggd.world/p/the-great-splintering-how-digital, accessed 10 February 2025.

19 "progressive algorithm", etc.: Thomas Mayo, "Young men and the far right's influence on them", *The Saturday Paper*, 21 December 2024.

20 "Now, individuals can be self-radicalised": Mike Burgess, in Daniel Keane, "ASIO chief Mike Burgess tells social media summit of 'disturbing resurgence' in youth terror cases", ABC News online, 11 October 2024.

20 "if necessary, feminism": Sara Meger, Melissa Johnston and Yolanda Riveros-Morales, *Misogyny, Racism and Violent Extremism in Australia*, Policy Brief, June 2024, Faculty of Arts, University of Melbourne.

23 "In short": Gary Barker et al., *State of American Men 2023: From crisis and confusion to hope*, Equimundo, Washington, 2023.

23 graphic videos of the Wakeley church stabbing: The video remained online, and the e-Safety Commission's advice was vindicated in the most horrible way imaginable: British teenager Axel Rudakubana sought out the footage forty minutes before he went on a stabbing rampage at a Taylor Swift–themed dance class in the UK, murdering three young girls and injuring eight.

23 "He issued a dog whistle": Jake Evans and Jordyn Butler, "eSafety drops case against Elon Musk's X over church stabbing videos", ABC News online, 5 June 2024.

23 Plan International Australia's Gender Compass: Plan International, *Gender Compass: A segmentation of Australia's views on gender equality*, Plan International Australia, 2023.

24 "We have a responsibility": Elena Campbell et al., "Unlocking the prevention potential: Accelerating action to end domestic, family and sexual violence", Rapid Review Expert Panel, Department of the Prime Minister and Cabinet, Canberra, 2024, p. 32.

25 "the sheer amount of confusion": Susanne Legena, "Gender Compass shows equality still some way to go", *The Canberra Times*, 18 September 2023.

26 "Intimate-partner homicides": Waleed Aly, *The Project*, 1 May 2025.

26 "We can't just wait": Annabelle David, *The Project*, 1 May 2025.

26 "showing encouraging signs": Our Watch, "Tracking progress in prevention and report card", Our Watch website, ourwatch.org.au/change-the-story/tracking-progress-in-prevention, accessed 10 February 2025.

28 "control the tools": Damon Beres, "Billions of people in the palm of Trump's hand", *The Atlantic*, 20 January 2025.

28 "The sense of disempowerment": Simon Welsh in Michelle Grattan, "Labor has to grapple with Anthony Albanese's 'man problem'", *Guardian Australia*, 17 January 2025.

28 "This literally": Annabelle Daniel in Kristine Ziwica, "Health authority suppressed gendered violence research," *The Saturday Paper*, 27 July 2024.

31 NCAS Youth Report: ANROWS, *Attitudes Matter: The 2021 National Community Attitudes towards Violence Against Women Survey findings for young Australians*, 2023, p. 27.

38 "one of the most crucial", "Delay on this issue": Patty Kinnersly, "Schools need to be front line of stopping violence against women", *The Canberra Times*, 11 November 2023.

39 "the single most important criterion": Sarah Kearney et al., *Respectful Relationships Education in Schools: The beginnings of change*, Final evaluation report, prepared for Department of Premier and Cabinet and Department of Education and Training, Victoria, Our Watch, 2016.

39 "a resurgent male supremacy": Stephanie Wescott, Steven Roberts and Xuenan Zhao, "The problem of anti-feminist 'manfluencer' Andrew Tate in Australian schools: Women teachers' experiences of resurgent male supremacy", *School of Education Culture & Society*, Vol. 36, No. 2, 2024.

39 "While sexual harassment": Stephanie Wescott and Steven Roberts, "Investigating the growing culture of misogyny in Australian schools", *AEUnews*, 28 July 2023, news.aeuvic.asn.au/in-depth/investigating-the-growing-culture-of-misogyny-in-australian-schools, accessed 14 February 2025.

39 one national survey: Maggie Dent, *Sexual Harassment of Teachers*, Collective Shout, 28 October 2024.

41 thirteen: Our Watch, "Impact of pornography on young people survey report summary", November 2024.

41 "I think he liked": Carmel Hobbs, *Young, In Love and In Danger: Teen domestic violence and abuse in Tasmania: Research report*, Anglicare, November 2022, p. 61.

41 seven out of ten: Our Watch, "Impact of pornography".

44 "There must be knowledge": "Flipping the script on campus sexual assault", *Ms.*, 7 November 2018, msmagazine.com/2018/07/11/flipping-script-campus-sexual-assault/, accessed 13 February 2025.

44 The bottom line: E.C. Lopez and M.P. Koss, "Comment on Porat et al. (2024): 'Preventing sexual biolence: A behavioral problem without a behaviorally informed solution'", *Psychological Science in the Public Interest*, Vol. 25, No. 1, 2024.

45 this meta-review did not find: Responding to the paper in a brief comment online, the activist and educator Jackson Katz said he was "troubled" by the review's "incomplete – and therefore misleading" discussion of the bystander approach. The program he created – Mentors in Violence Prevention – took a "gender transformative" approach, whereas many other bystander programs "chose to downplay or eliminate discussions about gender norms in an effort to avoid potential pushback from men." Suffice it to say, he wrote, there are many ways to do bystander training.

45 "There is little to no": Roni Porat et al., "Preventing sexual violence: A behavioral problem without a behaviorally informed solution", *Psychological Science in the Public Interest*, Vol. 25, No. 4, 2024.

46 at least four years later: Safe Dates evaluators note that the only published evaluations of the Safe Dates program have been in this rural US sample. Future studies are needed to determine the effectiveness of Safe Dates for adolescents living in other locales.

48 "common cause": In that same submission, the consortium also conceded there was limited evidence that primary prevention could prevent perpetration and victimisation, due to the lack of longitudinal evaluations (studies that track participants' behaviour over the longer term).

50 20 per cent: Barron, Kai et al., "Alcohol, violence and injury-induced mortality: Evidence from a modern-day prohibition", WZB Discussion Paper, No. SP II 2022-301, Wissenschaftszentrum Berlin für Sozialforschung (WZB), Berlin, 2022.

51 a ban on alcohol in Bihar: Suman Chakrabarti et al., "Effects of a large-scale alcohol ban on population-level alcohol intake, weight, blood pressure, blood glucose, and domestic violence in India: A quasi-experimental population-based study", *The Lancet Regional Health – Southeast Asia*, Vol. 26, 2024.

51 three-quarters in 2015: Mary P. Ross, "Alcohol is becoming more common in sexual assault among college students", *The Conversation*, 13 June 2022.

51 a known factor in 60 per cent: Australian Domestic and Family Violence Death Review Network and ANROWS, 'Australian Domestic and Family Violence Death Review Network national data update', *Australian Domestic and Family Violence Death Review Network Data Report*, 2nd edn, ANROWS, 2022.

51 review of almost 200 intimate-partner homicides: Hayley Boxall et al. *The "Pathways to Intimate Partner Homicide" Project: Key stages and events in male-perpetrated intimate partner homicide in Australia*, Research report, 04/2022, ANROWS, 2022.

51 alcohol played the most definitive role: Alcohol was also a factor, though not as common, in the other offender "pathways." For example, 31 per cent of "fixated threat" offenders (defined as extremely controlling but otherwise high- functioning) were intoxicated at the time of the murder.

52 highest rates of alcohol-fuelled domestic violence: Cassandra Hopkins et al., "Harm to children from others' drinking: A survey of caregivers in Australia", *Addiction Journal*, 27 August 2024.

52 one in six Australian children: Hopkins et al., "Harm to children".

53 "alcohol is a bomb": When alcohol triggers a rush of blood to our brain, it scrambles our prefrontal cortex (responsible for rational decision-making and impulse control). So we become more disinhibited, and less able to make accurate judgements. As the frontal cortex scrambles, the limbic system – the area involved in emotional processing – is also affected, creating greater potential for mood swings and anger. The brain chemical glutamate is also suppressed, which further impairs cognitive functioning and makes it hard to form memories. For the first few drinks, we feel pretty good – because alcohol initially increases dopa- mine levels. But as we get more intoxicated, our serotonin levels become depleted, and as serotonin helps us control our impulses and regulate our moods, a depletion of serotonin makes increased aggression more likely. See, for instance, Kajol V. Sontate et al., "Alcohol, aggression, and violence: From public health to neuroscience", *Frontiers in Psychology*, Vol. 12, 2021.

55 "alcohol and drug use masks": Department for Victorian Communities, 2003.

56 "Alcohol was destroying': Connie Clark, "To hell and back – how June Oscar dried out Fitzroy Crossing", *The Daily Telegraph*, 15 August 2016.

57 "We don't need": Helen Fejo-Frith in Keira Jenkins, "'We've got enough alcohol': Bagot Community continues fight against liquor megastore", *The Point*, 31 March 2021, sbs.com.au/nitv/the-point/article/weve-got-enough-alcohol-bagot- community-continues-fight-against-liquor-megastore/p3xk8p4k5, accessed 11 February 2025.

57 "Severe intoxication": Peggy O'Dwyer in Melissa Mackay, "Marcia Langton calls for 'no exceptions' alcohol restrictions in the NT during domestic violence inquiry", ABC News, 1 November 2023.

58 "For whatever reason" and "locked her": N. Hing et al., "Impacts of male intimate partner violence on women: A life course perspective", *International Journal of Environmental Research and Public Health*, Vol. 18, 2021.

59 postcodes in Victoria: F. Markam, B. Doran and M. Young, "The relationship between electronic gaming machine accessibility and police-recorded domestic violence: A spatio-temporal analysis of 654 postcodes in Victoria, Australia, 2005–2014", *Social Science and Medicine*, Vol. 162, 2016.

59 14 per cent of men: Aruna Sathanapally, Kate Griffiths and Elizabeth Baldwin, "A better bet: How Australia should prevent gambling harm", Grattan Institute, 4 September 2024.

60 "It seems the AFL": Tim Costello, "Gender-based violence, gambling and the hypocrisy of the AFL", Alliance for Gambling Reform, 10 May 2024, agr.org.au/news/gender-based-violence%2C-gambling-and-the-hypocrisy-of-the-afl, accessed 11 February 2025.

61 $12 billion: Aruna Sathanapally, Kate Griffiths and Elizabeth Baldwin, "A better bet: How Australia should prevent gambling harm", Grattan Institute, 2024.

64 counterintuitive statistics from Nordic countries: Enrique Gracia and Juan Merlo, "Intimate partner violence against women and the Nordic paradox", *Social Science & Medicine*, Vol. 157, 2016.

64 sexual assault: Some sceptics have questioned the validity of the statistics cited in the original paper on the Nordic paradox, especially questioning the methodology behind the 2014 FRA survey that formed the evidence base. However, high gendered violence prevalence rates have been recorded in several studies since, including in Sweden (Brottsförebyggande rådet or Brå for short [Brå], 2021), Denmark (Bertelsen et al., 2019), Finland (Lehti et al., 2019), Norway (Thoresen & Hjemdal, 2014), and Iceland (Skilbrei et al., 2019).

65 study in Nicaragua: Mary Ellsberg et al., "Long-term change in the prevalence of intimate partner violence: A 20-year follow-up study in León, Nicaragua, 1995–2016", *BMJ Global Health*, Vol. 5, No. 4, 2020.

65 "the evidence base on": Mary Ellsberg, Margarita Quintanilla & William J. Ugarte, "Pathways to change: Three decades of feminist research and activism to end violence against women in Nicaragua", *Global Public Health*, Vol. 17, No. 11, 2022.

71 three distinct pathways: Hayley Boxall et al., *The "Pathways to Intimate Partner Homicide" Project: Key stages and events in male-perpetrated intimate partner homicide in Australia*, Research report, 04/2022, ANROWS, 2022.

81 "almost non-existent", "I've tried", etc.: Hobbs, *Young, In Love and In Danger*, pp. 62, 44, 53, 40, 116.

83 It involved questions: The four questions for family violence were about: a) witnessing physical assault; b) witnessing serious threats of physical assault; c) witnessing damage to property or pets; and d) witnessing coercive control (verbal, sexual, financial or relational). For the most part, such things were witnessed multiple times.

84 Compared to older Australians: None of this abuse was sporadic or shortlived – it counted only if it continued over weeks, months or years.

85 more than 60 per cent: Divina M. Haslam et al., "The prevalence of corporal punishment in Australia: Findings from a nationally representative survey", *Australian Journal of Social Issues*, 24 November 2023.

85 permitting state-sanctioned violence: Corporal punishment is also linked to a higher likelihood of problems with mental and emotional health, lower self-esteem, more aggression and antisocial behaviour, higher rates of anxiety and depression, and a greater likelihood of substance abuse.

85 when this practice was first introduced: As documented in the SNAICC's *Growing Up Our Way: Child rearing practices matrix*, Aboriginal child-rearing was traditionally very gentle. Accounts from north Arnhem Land and the central desert region observed that Aboriginal parents "were much attached to the child and rarely punished or corrected them." Authoritarian practices were "entirely absent," with fathers more likely to "protect an unruly child from their mother's exasperation." Instead of harsh discipline, "humour, teasing and surprised responses are commonly used by adults or peers to indicate to children that their behaviour is undesirable or non-conformist." When Aboriginal people saw how the Europeans physically punished their own children, they were "aghast."

85 institutional child sexual abuse was radically reduced: Gabriele Hunt et al., 'The prevalence of child sexual abuse perpetrated by leaders or other adults in religious organizations in Australia', *Child Abuse & Neglect*, September 2024.

85 "huge change can happen": The flip side of this is, as Mathews emphasises, the mental health disorders and harms that persist for the higher percentage of Australians who experienced these forms of sexual abuse in the past, and that one in twenty-five Australians aged sixteen to twenty-four has been sexually assaulted by an adult family member: "roughly one in every Year 12 classroom in Australia."

90 As Gilligan outlines: James Gilligan, "Shame, guilt, and violence", *Social Research*, Vol. 70, No. 4, 2003.

90 "If a man believes": Jane Gilmore, "Rape is a theoretical crime: Part 4 – Why do men rape?", *Substack*, 12 December 2024.

95 "When we talk about violence" and "The mothers": Yumi Lee and Catherine Barrett in Kate Lyons, "Older women allegedly killed by family members a 'silent crisis', experts say", *Guardian Australia*, 27 January 2025.

102 For other children: Many children are removed for other reasons, and this risks starting a new cycle of violence, as discussed later in the essay.

103 double the national average: Catherine Liddle et al., *Family Matters Report 2024*, SNAICC, 2024.

108 "[They] just move me around like a doggy": Zoë Robinson, *Moving Cage to Cage: An interim report of the Special Inquiry into children and young people in alternative care arrangements*, Advocate for Children and Young People, 2024, p. 19.

MINORITY REPORT

Correspondence

Bill Kelty

> *"You're travelling through another dimension, a dimension not only of sight and sound but of mind. A journey into a wondrous land whose boundaries are that of imagination. That's the signpost up ahead – your next stop, the Twilight Zone."*
>
> Rod Serling, *The Twilight Zone*, Season 2, 1960–61

The world of politics is changing.

An entertainer businessman has taken over an entire political party in the United States, a feat never before achieved, not even by the greatest of US presidents past. The once-dominant Labor Party in Israel has been reduced to a rump. The Socialists of France, who not that long ago competed in and won presidential elections, are now bit players in a left-wing Opposition coalition. The Labour Party in the UK won office with a huge parliamentary majority in July 2024 despite receiving the lowest vote share of any majority party in British history; the Conservative Party received its lowest vote share ever.

In November 2024 a far-right presidential candidate in Romania achieved the highest share of the vote by using only TikTok and some outside assistance. It will no longer be a surprise if far-right parties win power in France and Germany, and third-party forces led by Farage in the UK challenge for real power. The Green parties' wave may not have developed into the general tsunami they hoped for, but they remain a cogent force for young people concerned with the environment.

Then there is a burgeoning China led by the world's biggest-ever Communist Party; a possible Putin-led victory for the Russians in Ukraine; and Donald Trump's New Deal for America. Woven together in Trump's promises to bring the United States back home and wage war on the "deep state" of his own country are his claims that climate change is a hoax, vaccines are unsafe and universal health care is socialism.

We are entering the Twilight Zone.

Set against this background, George Megalogenis's essay on the new shape of Australian politics is an incisive analysis of changing political structures. The 2025 Australian election will both mark the essay and judge the Albanese Labor government. If the government is returned with a similar or greater margin, the Labor team will be lauded as great tactical managers who took the nation through the post-COVID recovery with great competence, and George's essay will be quietly forgotten. If the government just hangs on or is in minority government territory, it will wear the badge of mediocrity trumping bravery and George's essay will gain a place in history for being right on the mark. If the LNP wins outright or gains the most seats, the Albanese government will have won a special place in history as the Labor Party's equivalent to the Liberal government of Billy McMahon – one of the worst governments in Australian history – and George's essay may have got the symptoms right but the cure wrong.

Megalogenis is absolutely right to describe a new shape of Australian politics. The major political parties' primary vote has fallen from over 90 per cent to a little over 66 per cent. It is thirty-five years since Bob Hawke won the 1990 election with 39.4 per cent of the primary vote. The Greens took votes from Labor only to give them back in preferences. The Democrats took votes from the Liberals. Of great relevance is the number of independents who recently took votes from all the major parties and did not have their preferences distributed because they won. The net result is more independents and minor parties in the House of Representatives. At sixteen, this is a record.

So what explains these shifts?

It is a bit of a puzzle as, after all, most Australians who own their own homes and have superannuation are rich. The historical national covenant that is Australia – the ALP as champion of great safety nets and the Liberals as agents for private contribution and personal effort – has served most of the nation well. This national covenant is under great pressure as wealth inequality spirals.

The major parties, either individually or collectively, have been responsible for the National Disability Insurance Scheme, Australia's retirement system, the highest minimum wages structure in the world and safely navigating two international crises in the global financial crisis (GFC) and COVID-19. The number of voters who are millionaires is the greatest in the nation's history. During the term of the Albanese government they've seen house prices continue to rise and the stock market increase by almost 20 per cent.

But there is a deeper question. Since the 2008–09 global financial crisis the annual value of Australian exports has increased by 165 per cent, or $325 billion – from just under $200 billion in 2009 to more than $520 billion in the year to

October 2024. In that time productivity has increased by 12 per cent, and our terms of trade have improved dramatically to record levels. So where has that wealth gone?

It hasn't gone to reduce government debt, because total government net debt has grown from a surplus of $39.3 billion in 2008–09 to a debt of $847.8 billion in 2023–24. In fairness, an increase in debt was vital in dealing with the two great challenges of the GFC and COVID. It hasn't gone to lower taxes, because PAYE/PAYG, the GST and HECS have all increased in real terms. It hasn't gone to increased wages, because average earnings have risen by just 0.5 per cent a year in real terms since 2009, have been flat since 2013 and have fallen by 6 per cent since 2019. It has not gone to improve Medicare, because the average patient contribution has more than doubled, having increased from $34.55 to $78.93. It hasn't gone to improve teachers' wages, because they have fallen dramatically in some states in real terms. It is hard to see any improvement in our defence capacity. And in the period we have seen a big increase in the number of women in poverty.

But …

The lowest paid have seen minor improvements and received the increase in the superannuation guarantee contribution. The pension has increased in real terms except for those aged under sixty-seven since the pension age was increased. The super guarantee charge has increased from 9 per cent to 11.5 per cent and the average annual industry-fund return has been 8 per cent per annum. The NDIS has been introduced and it is a remarkable addition to welfare. Employment has increased by a third, from 10.9 million to 14.5 million. Share market prices have increased by 90 per cent. The wealth of the nine richest people in Australia has increased fourfold, from $52 billion in 2011 to $206 billion in 2023. House prices have doubled.

In short, the increased wealth has gone to property owners, shareholders, the very rich, executives, retirees and some recipients of the NDIS. But Medicare is weaker, housing unaffordability is greater, real wages have barely moved, and if I hazard a guess our defence capacity is not much improved.

These outcomes do not come about by chance or bad luck. Constipating enterprise bargaining stops real wages rising. Freezing the payment to doctors increases the gap to be paid by the patients. Reducing the supply of public accommodation increases homelessness. Deferring superannuation increases reduces the democratic distribution of capital gains. Reducing the age of dependency for children from fourteen to eight forces more women into poverty. Wasting scores of billions of dollars on badly managed infrastructure forces up debt and inflation. Reducing competition in the banking sector increases costs and reduces the availability of capital for both consumers and small businesses. Increasing the age of retirement for women to sixty-seven but without equality in superannuation increases the burden on women. Increasing the tax on HECS compounds the unfairness that many young people face.

These have been discrete policy decisions enacted by parliaments at all levels. They have had real consequences. The truth is that both major political parties own these decisions and their outcomes. This is the wedge of despair. The people who are paying higher taxes, higher rents, higher mortgage interest rates and higher prices for daily necessities, and who do not have a share in the fastest growing bank in the land – the bank of Mum and Dad – are under great pressure.

At the same time the two major political groupings have developed a unified position on AUKUS and the treatment of refugees but have been unable or unwilling to have a similar pact on the issues of climate change and treatment of First Nations Australians. Both these issues are deeply resonant with large sections of the community, and both have been played for social division, filling the well of discontent with the major political parties. But they are not the only explanation.

The Liberal Party has cleansed itself of a great number of moderates. The Labor Party walked away from Hawke and Keating after the 1996 election and has regularly disenfranchised its members. Bill Shorten's campaign for ideas and ideals did not win government. Malcolm Turnbull, the moderate Liberal, was soon found wanting in a party where he probably did not belong. The Rudd and Gillard governments were beset by the GFC and internal squabbling.

There is something in a two-party system that is always challenging: they fight each other. Australian politics may not be the most brutal on Earth, but they do fight each other. They concentrate almost solely on one another because they are the heavyweight contestants. Muhammad Ali and Joe Frazier did each other no good.

Like the Rudd and Gillard governments, the Albanese government has done some very good things. It has improved the industrial relations legislation, put a bandage over a rupturing Medicare system, repaired the NDIS, improved wages for childcare workers and workers in the aged-care sector, and has seen employment rise and the rate of inflation fall. It has steered a saner and more mature approach to trading with China.

All of this ignores one glaring fact. The living standards of most working Australians have fallen. On a per capita basis, growth has been negative and productivity increases tiny. Housing unaffordability is at record levels. Notwithstanding the cost-of-living tax cuts, PAYE/PAYG taxes are now at record levels. Nearly every OECD nation has experienced a post-COVID jump in employment. Yet nearly every government has lost power, because living standards have been crushed by inflation due in large measure to geopolitical turmoil. At the same time the surge in migration correlates with the economic malaise. The Albanese government may be the first Labor government since James Scullin's that has not left working people better off at the end of its term than they were at the start.

If there is one document of doom, it is the OECD Employment Outlook report of June 2024. It concluded that the average increase since COVID in real wages in the OECD was 1.5 per cent. But it was far from universal:

Australia	–4.8%
Spain	–2.5%
Germany	–2.0%
USA	–0.8%

Employment Outlook 2024 – Country Notes; 2019 to 1st Quarter 2024

The latest reports have per capita GDP in Australia declining for seven consecutive quarters, with national income per person falling by $1660 in the past year alone.

The essential tests for political parties are measured by reality and hope. The reality is that many, if not most, people do not believe they are better off now than before the last election. Many are better off but the majority are not. To pass the second test requires advocacy, goodwill and imagination.

This leads to the Voice. It was a chance for Albanese to stand on a pedestal of history. Rudd said sorry and Albanese would give Indigenous Australians a constitutional Voice. Up to election night it was hard to believe that he carried a bright and burning light for Indigenous peoples' rights. Albanese had advised Shorten against a treaty, but this was the big news on election night. The Voice was a noble legal idea, not without merit, but it was a means, not an end. Keating had said to Troy Bramston, "I am not a supporter of the so-called constitutional route to recognition. The route to recognition has to be straight through the front door: with a document acknowledging prior occupation, including recognition and atonement for the dispossession. A treaty is the best way to do this, notwithstanding it has to be 200 years late. If my forebears had been here for 60,000 years, there is no way I would be fobbed off in this country's horse and buggy utilitarian constitution." But here they were being offered a cosy political cupboard to satisfy a very meagre request. When nobody could tell the country what was in the cupboard, the support fell off a cliff. Millions of generous and compassionate Australians gave powerful support to a scrap of an idea, and it failed. It was hardly surprising that the Indigenous community was split. Lidia Thorpe demanding a treaty and Jacinta

Nampijinpa Price demanding greater respect for tribal communities were both right. But the Voice did affect the Albanese government. It lost, its advocacy amounted to nothing, and it put back the argument for and prospect of a negotiated treaty. Shorten was proved to be right. The Voice was not the start of the process but had to be the result of a treaty process.

It is true that the decline in popularity for Albanese tracked the fate of the Voice, but it was not the cause. During every day of the debate, the living standards of Australians fell; every day many could not pay their bills, every day prices rose. The Voice debate did show that the prime minister was not Hawke or Keating, but everybody knew that anyway. The debate also showed that he was not a cunning and canny tactician like John Howard, but most people knew that as well.

The long-term damage was not losing the Voice but harming the prospects for a treaty process. The debate showed that Dutton was closer to Howard than Albanese was to Hawke. To make Nampijinpa Price the chief spokesperson in Opposition to the "Yes" vote was really smart. It should have taught everybody not to dismiss Dutton so readily as a future prime minister.

The difficulty Albanese faces is that the electorate is losing trust. The government's childcare policies are expansive and expensive, but are substantially lost in inflation; the housing fund policy is lost in disbelief and inadequacy, as not enough homes are being built. It is as simple as that. The Future Made in Australia Innovation Fund appears to be entrepreneurial, but its outcomes are unclear and untested. The trouble is that the government can pick winners and losers. At the same time, Australia seems to have a real problem building homes, roads, tunnels and railways, and, for that matter, keeping submarines submerged and operating.

The latest budget papers set out a vision for many people that is frightening. A modicum of an increase in real wages, a continuing shortage of homes, a higher proportion of taxes paid by PAYE/PAYG taxpayers, moderate or low growth, negligible productivity growth and Medicare under great pressure.

The Albanese government can claim to be a good manager in reducing the deficit, reducing inflation and increasing employment. But putting up your hand for being a good economic manager during a period of government that has seen the living standards of workers crippled is to make Ebenezer Scrooge the hero of *The Christmas Carol*. It just doesn't wash.

It is true that the next election will not be easy for the ALP to win.

George's essay is optimistic that a minority government will bring renewed hope for inspirational ideas. That cause for optimism can be confirmed by the quality of some of the politicians from the non-major political parties. The Greens' Sarah Hanson-Young, Nick McKim and Barbara Pocock, the independents Jacqui

Lambie, Helen Haines, David Pocock and Bob Katter, and some of the teals are giving life to a tired old place.

Optimists should always be encouraged but the reality is that few minority governments in the world have proved to be great governments. The ACT government is a good example of good practical people working together. The Gillard minority government and the pact in Tasmania are not good examples for the Labor Party, the Greens or the independents. The political system creates diversity in the Senate but still promotes an essentially binary choice in the House of Representatives.

It is hard to see any minority government turning around AUKUS, establishing a common front on climate change, developing a treaty with Indigenous Australians, initiating tax reform of substance, improving productivity, delivering greater equality in the distribution of wealth or producing a new manifesto for the young.

AUKUS may collapse under the weight of its own stupidity. For the rest, the Labor Party will need to offer a clear strategy for young people that demonstrates that Labor is on their side; argues for a fairer tax system; seeks for parliament to lead on climate change; proves they will build the homes; doesn't pick sides in an economic contest between the United States and China; fights for Medicare; and shows that Australia can be a modern economy. This is what is needed to keep hope alive.

The Liberal–National Coalition can win. They need to win one more seat than the ALP and more votes overall. With such an outcome, no amount of posturing will deny them the right to form government. Dutton should not be underestimated. He will have more financial support than any Liberal leader for a hundred years if the love affair with the politics of Palmer, Rinehart and others continues.

We may confront a reality that – with AUKUS and nuclear plants – the Liberal government proposes the biggest socialist investment in this country's history. Don't be surprised if neither eventuates, but if they do perhaps a trillion dollars will be needed. That is all the savings for most of the working people in this country for decades. It will be working people who will pay the price for generations.

Australia will never be the same.

Anything can happen in the Twilight Zone.

Bill Kelty

MINORITY REPORT

Correspondence

Sam Roggeveen

In *Minority Report*, George Megalogenis marks the 2010 election as the end of Australia's two-party system. It was "the last campaign run on the old 40–40–20 rule, whereby the duopoly typically garnered at least 80 per cent of first-preference votes between them." Twelve years and four elections later, at the 2022 poll, "the primary vote divided into a third each for Labor, the Coalition and none of the above." A continuation of this trend at the upcoming election "would make the none-of-the-above vote the largest bloc of the three."

It is striking how little consideration the decline of Australia's major parties gets in our political commentary, even though its bleak implications for Labor and the Liberal–National Coalition are obvious. At the 2022 election, Labor won with 32.6 per cent of the primary vote, its lowest since 1934, prompting journalist Andrew Probyn to write, "In any other decade, this would be a result that triggers talk of an existential crisis." The Coalition is faring little better.

Megalogenis has drawn welcome attention to this shift, but even he may be understating its significance. In fairness, Megalogenis casts his analysis explicitly around the upcoming federal election, so, having declared the scope of his enquiry, he can't be faulted for failing to go beyond it. But the end of the duopoly doesn't just promise to deliver another minority government in 2025. It is unravelling the political settlement that has prevailed in Australia since the Liberal Party was formed in 1944.

Let's note that we have no idea whether major-party decline has hit its floor in Australia. The share of the primary vote enjoyed by the duopoly has fallen steadily since the 1970s, and it is not obvious why the decline should stop now. We shouldn't be thinking only about another minority government after the next election but about minority government becoming a permanent feature of Australian federal politics.

So, what happened? Perhaps the best guide to understanding this phenomenon is the Irish political scientist Peter Mair, who charted a similar decline in major-party popularity in Western Europe from the 1950s to the 2000s. Democracy, he concluded, was hollowing out. Citizens were pulling back from the democratic process and, in response, the major parties were staging a retreat of their own.

The nineteenth and early twentieth centuries marked the rise of mass movements in politics – parties, trade unions, citizen armies, churches, professional associations. But by the second half of the twentieth century, this trend was exhausted and Western democracies saw a slow deterioration in mass politics – ordinary citizens stopped joining political parties and politics-adjacent organisations.

Thanks largely to communications technology, election campaigns became less labour-intensive and more capital-intensive, so donors mattered more than members (indeed, smaller memberships were easier to control). Politics was becoming the domain of professionals. In the Australian Labor Party, this process was described pungently by Kim Beazley Snr as a transition from the cream of the working class to the scum of the middle class. But all big parties were moving in the same direction, as were protest and lobbying groups.

As the need for members declined and that for funding grew, the Hawke Labor government legislated in 1984 for public financial support of election campaigns. This was very much in line with trends in Europe, leading Mair to observe that whereas political parties were once a way for the public to talk to the state, now they were becoming a way for the state to talk to the public. "The age of party democracy has passed," Mair wrote. "Although the parties remain, they have become so disconnected from the wider society … that they no longer seem capable of sustaining democracy in its present form."

We are left with a hollow democracy. Megalogenis quotes former Labor grandee Bill Kelty's pitiless judgement on the modern ALP, which he describes as stale, ambitionless and "mired in mediocrity." It's a verdict Megalogenis extends to the Liberals. The party decline thesis readily explains this torpor. For one thing, as membership declines in the major parties, so does the leadership talent available to them. Disconnection from the public also robs the party of opportunities to learn what the public wants and cares about.

But perhaps most importantly, when political parties cease to represent a large and coherent social and economic base, their sense of authority erodes. To put it simply, they no longer feel like they're really in charge. To make up for the authority deficit, governments at all levels and across the ideological spectrum embark on the manic pursuit of consultation. Either that or they seek authority from semi-political or semi-judicial institutions that enjoy higher public trust than they do:

the Reserve Bank, royal commissions, the Fair Work Commission, the Foreign Investment Review Board and so on.

If there's an optimistic way to look at our predicament, it is by asking: compared to what? You say Australia is a mess. Compared to what? You think our politicians are mendacious, untrustworthy, incompetent, corrupt. Compared to what? You say the economy is performing poorly. Compared to what? Australians typically believe they are led by fools, yet there is hardly a better governed country in the world.

The pessimistic reading is that the worst is yet to come, that the void which has opened between the public and the political class will only widen. Whether federal, state or local, you would not find a single politician in Australia who does not loudly proclaim their support for democracy. All of them believe in universal suffrage, free elections, free speech and freedom of assembly. But ask yourself: how many of those same politicians want *more* democracy? What significant figure or constituency in Australian political life proposes to surrender political power to the public?

Megalogenis concludes that "a hung parliament offers perhaps our last best chance to restore purpose to our politics – and policymaking." I hope he's right, but the teals and other crossbenchers have no more claim on our loyalty than the major parties do. They, too, are operating in the aftermath of mass-movement politics.

The duopoly represents an idea of Australia which no longer applies: we are post-industrial, post-union, post–Cold War. The neoliberal policy agenda that sustained the major parties since the 1980s is exhausted, the workplace feminised, the old media in decline, our great ally diminished by domestic dysfunction and a new foreign rival. Maybe that's why our present moment feels both stagnant and charged with possibility. The existing political settlement is dying before our eyes, yet we have no inkling of what will replace it.

Sam Roggeveen

MINORITY REPORT

Correspondence

Judith Brett

The big question about the outcome of the election due before mid-May 2025 is whether it will result in a hung parliament. Writing this at the end of January, a Labor minority government looks the most likely outcome. Labor, which is flagging in the polls, only has to lose three seats to lose its majority, but the Coalition has to win twenty-one to form government. And whatever happens in the House of Representatives, neither is likely to control the Senate.

Megalogenis expresses cautious optimism about such an outcome. It represents, he writes, "our last best chance to restore purpose to our politics." I am always wary of historical ultimatums, but I agree with his cautious optimism. The major parties – the duopoly, as Megalogenis calls them – which have shared power since 1910, would have Australians believe that minority government is evidence of political dysfunction and will be weak and ineffective. But our history tells us they can be productive.

My evidence here is not the mishap-prone government of Julia Gillard, which faced an intransigent, misogynist Opposition, but the governments of Alfred Deakin in the first decade of the new Commonwealth. His second term of government, from July 1905 to November 1908, was enormously productive. A few of its achievements: tariffs to protect Australian industries; determining the site for the new capital after a great deal of political jockeying; establishing a Commonwealth Literary Fund and beginning Australian support for Antarctic exploration; expanding the High Court from three to five judges; beginning the transcontinental railway; passing the *Surplus Revenue Act*, which made possible the first Commonwealth welfare measure – the old age and invalid pension; laying the foundation of Australia's system of naval defence; establishing a pro rata system for the dispersal of Commonwealth funds to the states; and much more. All while leading a minority government.

For much of this he depended on the support of the Labor Party, and sometimes on members of the official Opposition or on independents. Support was not automatic, the result of an agreement, but rather was built for each piece of legislation through discussion, negotiation and compromise. This, said Deakin, was a good thing: it meant that his government's legislation represented wider experience than could be represented by just one party. When Labor won majority government in 1910 it built on much of the previous government's policies, because it had contributed to their formation.

After 1910 our party system took on the Labor versus non-labour shape we are now familiar with. The Country Party, which formed in 1920, introduced competing interests on the non-labour side, minor parties came and went, and non-labour reformed twice until the formation of the Liberal Party in 1944. But the basic shape remained the same until the end of the twentieth century, when the vote for candidates outside the duopoly started to increase and party identification to decline. In May 2022, a third of the electorate cast their primary vote for a non-major-party candidate. If this trend continues, as Megalogenis says, at the next election the non-major-party vote would be the largest bloc.

How are we to understand this situation? Megalogenis describes it as "a fractured electorate," a metaphor which implies that what was once whole is now broken, with new rifts and faultlines crisscrossing the older ones of class and region, which had once organised the parties' electoral support. This is true as far as it goes, but I would like to suggest another factor at play: the hollowing-out of our political parties as their membership has declined and they have become professional electoral machines.

To be sure, Australian society is more socially and culturally complex than it was in 1944 when Menzies formed the Liberal Party, but there were still plenty of conflicts of interests and values that had to be negotiated in the formation of policy. Much of this took place inside the parties as they determined the policies to put to the electorate. This was where debate, negotiation and compromise took place and when the legislation reached the parliament it was assured safe passage by the government's majority. With active memberships much larger than they are today, these debates connected with the lived experience, interests and prejudices of a range of electors. As the parties have become more professionalised and membership has declined, this connection to the electorate has atrophied.

Nothing shows this more clearly than the colossal failure of both sides of politics on housing policy and the disconnect between the housing riches of members of parliament and younger Australians who fear a lifetime of renting. The Greens' victories in Brisbane have finally shocked Labor into action, but it is cautious and Albanese's purchase of a $4.3-million house shows he doesn't really get it.

What is happening, I think, is that the debate, negotiation and consensus-building is shifting from inside the parties back to the parliament, where they were for most of the nineteenth and early twentieth centuries. Debates and their resolution still take place within the parties, but they are no longer as definitive. This process started in 1981, with the revitalisation of the Senate by the Australian Democrats. Since then, apart from John Howard from 2004 to 2007, no government has had a Senate majority and all have had to negotiate to pass their legislation. With a minority government, this process would start in the House of Representatives. The conflicts of interest will be more publicly visible than they are when the resolution takes place inside the parties. This will be a magnet for media speculation and give the impression of dysfunction, but in my opinion it is no cause for alarm. The public will have a clearer view of the interests and arguments at play, and the government will have to negotiate. But it does not mean the end of effective legislation.

It does mean, though, that the established players will have to learn. The ALP needs to learn how to cooperate with the Greens in particular, and the Greens need to become less intransigent. The Coalition needs a more complex understanding of the nation it aspires to govern. Peter Dutton projects only two images of the nation – one divided and weak under Labor, the other strong and united under him. It is a binary, black-and-white imaginary which fits awkwardly with the complexity of contemporary Australia and the parliament we are likely to have after the forthcoming election.

Judith Brett

MINORITY REPORT

Correspondence

Ben Raue

Thanks to George Megalogenis for writing such an illuminating essay. Too often political analysis focuses on the current shape of politics without enough perspective to see where things have come from or where they might be going.

One element that is usually missing from this sort of analysis is the role of the electoral system in shaping our party system. Most Australian parliaments are elected using a single-member majoritarian electoral system for their lower houses, usually alongside a proportional upper house. Supporters of a single-member electoral system will often claim it provides stable and responsible government by ensuring the election of single-party governments and pushing most voters to support one of the two major parties. But the single-member system no longer delivers this in Australia: support for independents and minor parties has boomed despite their chances of victory being minimised, and we've now reached a point where many seats in the House of Representatives are being won by minor parties and independents. It is becoming harder for either Labor or the Coalition to win majority government with the current shape of the party system.

Support for major parties in Australia reached its peak in the decade from the creation of the Liberal Party in the 1940s until the Labor split and the creation of the DLP in the 1950s. The major-party vote has mostly been on a downward trend since then, but for most of that time the electoral contest for the House of Representatives remained very much two-sided. If you wished to vote for a minor party in the House, you could comfortably do so and then preference a major party, and in almost every case it was that major-party preference that really mattered. The proportional Senate and preferential voting gave minor parties a role in the system, but they were kept away from centre-stage.

When Ted Mack won a seat in the House of Representatives in 1990, he was the first member of the House crossbench in over twenty years. Indeed, only one independent had won a seat in the House between 1949 and 1987. Even after Mack's win, it was rare to live in a seat that wasn't dominated by a Labor–Coalition contest. Between 1990 and 2007, only three to six seats at each election had a final preference count that wasn't a contest between the major parties.

Throughout this era, major parties could rest easy that voters who moved to a minor party or an independent would come back to them as preferences. That remained true until those other groupings became big enough to win seats – the Greens and teals have both crossed that threshold. Others may do so in the future.

While these groups were locked out of the House, they were able to win seats in the Senate. But the serious threat they pose in the House has created a different dynamic, which explains a lot of the difficulties the Labor government has had in the Senate. This Senate is not like the one Kevin Rudd faced after his first election. Labor and the Greens only held thirty-seven seats, with the only two other crossbenchers being centrist Nick Xenophon and religious conservative Steve Fielding. There was no option to do deals with the Greens, because they couldn't deliver enough votes to pass legislation. This is a detail rarely mentioned in the context of the defeat of the Carbon Pollution Reduction Scheme in 2009. It was only in 2011, after the senators elected in 2004 were cleared out, that the parties of the left held a clear Senate majority.

The clearly progressive parties could have similarly fallen short in 2022 but achieved a clear majority due to two unprecedented results: David Pocock's victory over the Liberal Party in the Australian Capital Territory, and Labor winning a third Senate seat in traditionally right-leaning Western Australia. This meant that together Labor, the Greens and progressive teal Pocock had a clear majority. Plus the two Jacqui Lambie Network senators were closer to this majority than Fielding had been in 2008.

So many of the challenges the current government faces in the Senate arise from incentives created by the single-member electorate system in the House that push Labor and the Greens away from being able to agree on legislation. Of course, Labor and the Greens disagree on plenty and some of those disagreements are fundamental. But there is also plenty on which there is room to come to an agreement. But the nature of competition for single-member electorates, and the lack of any kind of governing arrangement, make it harder.

When you look at an electorate where Labor and the Greens are competing to win the seat, a lot of the difference doesn't come down to a particular policy issue but to different theories of change: how you have an impact on a government. The Labor case is built on having the right people who can get things done; in many of these seats they argue that having a particular progressive champion inside the government is crucial to achieving left-wing policies. The Greens' case is built on being free to criticise from the outside, arguing that a Labor government is more likely to pay attention to the progressive causes popular in these sorts of electorates if they are at risk of losing the seat, or indeed do lose the seat. The Greens argue that a Labor government is more likely to pay attention to the left if it elects members who loudly criticise and force it to pay attention to those sorts of seats.

This theory explains why voters of similar demographics vote strongly for Adam Bandt in Melbourne and Anthony Albanese in Grayndler. It also explains why many of the same voters are solid for Tanya Plibersek in Sydney, Greens MPs in the overlapping state seats and independent Clover Moore for lord mayor. For swing voters, the different theories of change make more sense depending on the political context and the candidates.

Because of this conflict, Labor and the Greens aren't just attempting to achieve particular legislative outcomes – they are also competing to get the credit. Labor's case for winning those Labor/Greens marginals relies on its claim to be the only party that can achieve legislative change. The Greens' case relies on them being able to demonstrate they can make a difference by improving Labor's legislation and pushing it to do things that were not part of its plan.

So when legislation is presented to the Senate, you get an extended process of posturing – Labor members insisting that they are not willing to change the legislation, while the Greens issue their demands. It's not that there aren't real policy disagreements underlying this conflict, but the incentives of the electoral system push the parties away from each other. Ultimately, there remains a reason to get something done at the end, but they don't always get to that point.

The winner-takes-all nature of single-member electorates, which increases the importance of a handful of seats where the parties compete, rather than encouraging them to attract votes across the country, pushes the parties into this conflict, in a way that is less common under proportional electoral systems like that in the ACT. It also partly explains why these issues were less of a problem under previous governments with the Australian Democrats, who didn't make much progress in competing for seats in the House.

The single-member system is also becoming volatile and less predictable as the major-party vote declines. In the future, we could see parties winning large seat numbers off relatively low votes, and a worsening relationship between how people vote and who is elected. If a lot more seats start to look like Macnamara, with small changes in votes producing dramatically different results, election results may not have the legitimacy of selecting the clear winner.

There were two localised examples in 2022 where a party with a small share of the vote won most of the seats in an area. In the inner city of Brisbane, the

Greens polled 30.7 per cent of the primary vote and won all three seats. In the northern suburbs of Sydney, teal candidates polled 32.2 per cent across four electorates. They won three of those seats and came close in the fourth. Yet in both cases, a small swing could see the Brisbane Greens or the teals of northern Sydney without any seats. These volatile patterns could become more common if current trends continue.

I also appreciated Megalogenis's interesting comparison between the 1999 republic referendum and the 2023 Voice referendum. While seventeen Liberal seats voted "Yes" in 1999, just one – Bradfield – voted "Yes" in 2023. This is not because these seats were much less favourable to the Voice – these areas still mostly voted "Yes" in 2023 – but because most of them are no longer Liberal seats.

I find the comparison most interesting if you look past who won each seat and instead look at the relative trend. The "Yes" votes in 1999 and 2023 correlate very strongly, and also strongly with the Labor two-party-preferred vote in 2022. But the 1999 republic referendum result did not correlate very well with two-party-preferred. Looking back a quarter-century, the voting patterns of the 1999 republic referendum showed us where federal voting trends were heading: the Coalition losing ground in affluent inner-city areas and solidifying its hold on rural areas.

In the lead-up to the 2004 federal election, there was a lot of chatter about "doctors' wives" in affluent Liberal-voting electorates leaving the Liberal Party and voting for Labor, the Greens or the Democrats over issues such as climate change and refugees. This did not play out at the time, but with the benefit of twenty years' hindsight these predictions now look more premature than wrong.

When you look at the teal wave of 2022 through this historical lens, it is harder to see a dramatic reversal in this trend. The Liberal Party did not lose these inner-city seats simply because Scott Morrison alienated the base – rather, it was the culmination of decades of political change. I doubt this trend has finished playing out.

For this reason, I am sceptical about the comparison between the teals and the rural independents who supported the Gillard government in 2010 and then went on to retire in the face of expected defeat in 2013. Tony Windsor and Rob Oakeshott won their electorates in 2010 by large margins, but the Nationals still overwhelmingly won the two-party-preferred vote, with 67 per cent in New England and 62 per cent in Lyne. By contrast, Labor polled at least 44 per cent of the two-party-preferred vote in all but one of the teal seats, polling over 48 per cent in North Sydney and Warringah. Indeed, Labor won the two-party-preferred vote in Mayo. These teal areas are not solid conservative electorates like the rural seats that elected independents in 2010, and I don't think it would be as controversial for the members representing these areas to support a minority Labor government. Affluent inner-city areas have been fleeing the Liberal Party rapidly over the last quarter-century, and it is not obvious that their representatives should support the Liberal Party in a hung parliament.

Ben Raue

MINORITY REPORT

Correspondence

Peter Lewis

I read George Megalogenis's Quarterly Essay between sessions of the Melbourne Boxing Day Test cricket, a colonial artefact that has been transformed since becoming the world's most populous nation's number one sport. No longer supplicant, the Indian players are multimillionaires whose fortunes are tied to their mastery of a truncated form of the game, where five days' flow is compressed into a few hours of nonstop action. Australia has adapted to this new reality; a teenager on debut walked onto the MCG to play an innings that would have been inexplicable a decade ago, the crazy-brave ramp shots against the world's best bowler presaging a pulsating contest that enthralled for the best part of a week. I found myself immersed in a game that had reinvented itself while maintaining fidelity to its core values, history and traditions.

This transformation provided a poignant backdrop to George's essay, which takes the reader outside the day-to-day cut and thrust of politics to provide a helicopter view of the Albanese government's first test. His highlights reel includes the failed Voice referendum, the stage-three tax cuts backflip and the ongoing struggle to land a housing policy worthy of the name. These all play out against the backdrop of declining global conditions, as post-pandemic inflation drives a sullen, simmering rejection of the status quo. George portrays a government led by a skilled player currently struggling to find his political sweet spot.

Essential's polling over the life of this parliament reinforces George's core proposition: an ongoing drift from major parties; a growing number of people seeing no difference between them; and a contradictory desire for government to intervene more assertively along with a simultaneous lack of faith that such intervention will make any material difference. Add in the increasing number of people professing to be under financial pressure and a majority who feel the nation is heading in the wrong direction and this creates a dire environment for an incumbent party seeking to renew its mandate.

But beyond the day-to-day political contest, there are broader challenges for those in power. The impact of technological change, particularly the business models of Silicon Valley, has altered the nature of liberal democratic politics every bit as profoundly as Twenty20 has changed cricket. Both elected representatives and the remnants of the twentieth-century media have fallen captive to the logic of the digital platform business model, where conflict begets attention, which begets data, which begets income. None of it begets a sense of common purpose or fosters the sober reflection that drives consensus.

Corrosive hyper-conflict has become a feature, not a bug, of our politics, undermining any sense of common purpose – in politics, in media, in our social connections. There has formed a political big bash of weaponised snippets, images, hits of dopamine, where we get drawn into the game and, like one-eyed fanatics, cheer our team, boo the enemy, cry foul at the umpire. To be clear, a degree of conflict in any system is important, as it draws out much-needed complexity. But there needs to be a baseline of shared values for the system to function. When politics starts and ends at the point of conflict, we fail to see the humanity in each other; we cast moral judgement on those with different views. We seek not just to win a debate but to humiliate our opponents. And they to us. The victories we do achieve become ephemeral because they rely on the outcome of the contest rather than genuine consensus.

These factors combine to put pressure on the model of liberal democracy that emerged as the purest expression of individual freedom in the nineteenth century over the tyranny of the elite. Fewer people trust late-stage capitalism to act in their interests, a totally rational response to the lived experience of widening inequality and generational cleavages. Erstwhile progressive parties created to address these flaws have become synonymous with these failings and are seen as complicit apologists for a rotten system. Unsurprisingly, people are turning to alternatives. George rightly points out that, unlike in the United States and UK, where politics has been corralled by disenfranchised and disenchanted outsiders, the significant shift in Australia's past cycle has been the rise of moderate liberal independents, who have disrupted the binary contest for power by demanding something better that always seems just out of grasp.

In discussing the failure of the Voice referendum, George generously notes a *Guardian* column I wrote last year. At the time I described the post-referendum silence as a "quiet … so deafening it seemed to take on a form of its own; like the pall that descends on a dressing room after a heavy defeat, or the emptiness when a relationship fails." We had just conducted exploratory focus groups talking to those who had shifted from "Yes" to "No" during the campaign. These were not people who could easily be dismissed as racist; their inclination was to support First Nations people but they shifted when exposed to the noise and confected confusion of the "No" case driven by a media cycle insatiable for the next point of conflict. No one regretted their decision; in fact, by August 2024 the "No" vote had hardened.

As George notes, it would be easy to interpret the referendum result as a broader repudiation of "identity" politics at a time when people are focused on their personal financial circumstances. But this is only part of the explanation. The simple proposition that was rejected was to embed a formal and representative mechanism for First Nations peoples to provide input on decisions that affected them. This was successfully portrayed by those who opposed the Voice as "special rights and privileges" that other Australians do not enjoy. In a separate poll question Essential found that only big business is perceived to be listened to by government, with Indigenous Australians ranking higher than people with disability, small business, regional communities and "ordinary" Australians when it comes to being heard. The idea of being heard by government was deemed a form of special treatment.

The public's alienation from government is particularly challenging for progressive parties, where the social licence for change is critical. We have witnessed through the vexed rollout of renewable energy projects how fragile a shared consensus can be. I think this goes beyond the day-to-day challenges of a progressive government riding the wild horses of power, squeezed by the established vested interests. It starts with finding ways to privilege common purpose over the gravitational pull of maximum friction that I have described. In the mid-twentieth century, when most Australian employees were union members, the link between the industrial and political wings of the labour movement helped provide an anchor point. Today fewer people join things; John Kenneth Galbraith's notion of countervailing power has been eroded as we become constituencies of one.

In his concluding observations, George predicts an increase in influence for independents and hopes this will help "keep our politics anchored in the problem-solving centre." Absent positive reform to the way politics is conducted, I fear this is wishful thinking. In our current civic environment, it's no longer enough to play politics within the game; the real leadership challenge is to design how the contest will be played next season, and the one after that and the one after that. To torture the cricketing metaphor, our public spaces need groundstaff to ensure our discourse can be conducted safely, with true bounce to allow a genuine contest of ideas.

The good news is there are alternative civic models emerging that use pro-social technology to build on the foundations of liberal democracy. Some of us are taking inspiration from the work of Taiwan's first digital minister, Audrey Tang, a nonbinary hacker who adapted the knowhow of Silicon Valley to the 2012 Taiwanese demonstrations, where a proposed free trade deal with China was quashed and replaced with a citizens' charter. Under Tang's stewardship, trust in government rose from single figures to the high eighties, in part due to the world's most successful response to Covid without lockdowns, supported by a network of citizen journalists and fact checkers who identify and deprioritise mainland misinformation without blocking it – a constant normalising of the citizen voice. Whether Taiwan is a unicorn limited by its time and place in history or the maker of something that could be more widely applied remains to be seen.

There are some green shoots emerging locally as well. NewDemocracy has been building models of citizen juries for more than a decade. The corporate-backed Amplify project is hosting its first public deliberation in early 2025. And the government has funded the Disability Dialogue to build an independent space outside formal power structures. US not-for-profit New Public is working with public broadcasters, including the ABC, to build non-commercial digital spaces that could become a future public square. No single response will provide a silver bullet, but normalising innovation and risk-taking in citizen engagement, based around building points of common purpose and understanding, might be our best bet to reinvent a politics that speaks to the times while remaining true to our social- democratic traditions.

Back on the couch, I'm wondering if the ultimate test for Labor, should it cobble together another working term, is as structural as that the Australian team is confronting: how to not just play the game of democracy but have a serious crack at updating its infrastructure. I'm not talking about another quixotic attempt at constitutional change, which would inevitably be defeated; more a renovation of the practices of government to mitigate our current civic atrophy. The list of systemic issues demanding government attention is long: the first serious reform of privacy laws for forty years; licensing of social media platforms to ensure they comply with local laws; deep thinking on how to ensure AI works for the many, not the few. None of these issues can simply be "solved" by good policy; responses need to be designed to embrace ongoing citizen engagement as rapid changes in technology demand vigilance and resolve. Left to the current process, they will be shaped to fit the interests of those with the most money and access to power, further driving the resentment that threatens the stability of our system. As one of the architects of modern social liberal democracy, Labor seems uniquely placed to shepherd through these changes by reimagining civic participation while remaining true to the principles of social democracy.

Peter Lewis

MINORITY REPORT | Correspondence

Joel Deane

I have an unproven theory: Bob Hawke is to blame for Australia's inability to hold an informed debate on national reform.

That's the harebrained, tabloid-style headline, anyway. Here's the nuanced version.

In 1986, the Hawke government allowed Rupert Murdoch's News Limited to purchase The Herald and Weekly Times. Back then, the HWT was the largest media player in Australia, owning TV channels in Adelaide and Melbourne, several radio stations and fifteen newspapers. Under cross-media ownership rules, Murdoch couldn't hang onto the TV channels and radio stations but kept the newspapers.

That deal was a turning point in Australian public life, handing Murdoch control of 70 per cent of the nation's print media. Writing in *Media Information Australia* in 1990, former Fraser government minister Ian Macphee warned:

> Whilst we have yet to experience the blatantly one-sided media coverage of Mr Murdoch's earlier days, I am certain it will eventually occur and on a scale much larger than that witnessed in 1975 federally … Australian politicians have betrayed the basic freedom of our democracy. They have so corrupted the political process that they and their successors are and will continue to be intimidated by, and beholden to, a dwindling band of unaccountable media owners.

Macphee was right, but he missed something. Thanks to Hawke, Murdoch didn't just gain control of the vast majority of Australian print media, he also gained control of the vast majority of Australian journalists.

Before 1987, most Australian journos had not grown up in a Murdoch newsroom. After 1987, the vast majority of Australian journalists were either trained in or came up the ranks in News Limited newsrooms. That's not a criticism of the Murdoch journos; I know many fine journalists with a News Limited pedigree. But – and this is important – there was a relative diversity of publishing experience among journos before the HWT deal. Since then, the bloodlines of Australian journalism have thinned – alarmingly. And Australian media culture is so homogenised that most newsrooms are a variation of News Limited's blokey, knee-jerk, punitive culture. As a result, non-Murdoch media increasingly looks, sounds and reads like News Limited. Australian media is Murdoch media.

In case you're wondering, yes, I do blame Hawke for the state of Australian media. Bob was the prime minister who first bent the knee to Rupert – everything flows from that betrayal. Don't get me wrong, Australian journalism wasn't perfect before 1987, but there was more diversity.

All of which brings me to George Megalogenis's *Minority Report*.

George is right. The global financial crisis did trigger an anti-incumbent 'supercycle' in our politics and Anthony Albanese is likely to be leading a minority government by May. And that's the best scenario.

The good news is that the machinery of Australian democracy – unlike that of the United States or the United Kingdom – is geared towards the sensible centre, with compulsory voting rewarding campaigns that pitch to undecided voters rather than to the extremes of left or right. The political arrival of the teal independents proves this point. Fundamentally, Zali Steggall, Allegra Spender, Monique Ryan, Kate Chaney, Zoe Daniel and Sophie Scamps are all practical politicians. If, as George predicts, the teals hold the balance of power after the 2025 federal election, they are likely to back social, economic and environmental policies that are practical and progressive.

Why, then, am I so nervous about the aftermath of the next federal election?

For brevity, I'll confine myself to three reasons. First, there is the Donald Trump factor. We have no idea how the Australian electorate will react to the election of a crypto-fascist US president. Anything could happen. Second, as a group, Australia's federal politicians have not earned their keep since the turn of the century. Yes, there are exceptions – such as the handling of the GFC and the establishment of the National Disability Insurance Scheme – but, overall, Canberra has failed to value-add to the Federation. Third, Australia's media – homogenised by Murdoch – has also been severely weakened by the content theft of aggregators such as Google and the atomisation of audiences by social media. As a result, even if our media wanted to explain climate change, there is no longer a national audience available to hear that explanation.

Put it this way. Other than during the Olympics, Australia has forgotten to think, plan and act like a nation.

Joel Deane

John Quiggin

In his generally excellent Quarterly Essay, George Megalogenis asserts that "Rudd and Gillard do not have a policy reform legacy which survived the retribution of the Abbott government, apart from the National Disability Insurance Scheme." This is way off the mark. In reality, and despite their chaotic personal rivalry, Kevin Rudd and Julia Gillard achieved a good deal more than the NDIS, and most of it survived the nine subsequent years of LNP government. The big exceptions were carbon pricing and, arguably, the Gonski reforms.

Against these there is a substantial record of sustained achievement. First, and contrasting sharply with Anthony Albanese's failure on the Voice, Rudd delivered a historic Apology to Australia's Indigenous Peoples. At the same time, he introduced Welcome to Country as part of the opening of every parliament. This has become a well-established custom for all Australian public events. An attempt to challenge it in the wake of the Voice failure went nowhere.

On climate, Rudd ratified the Kyoto Protocol, which Howard had refused to sign. The Rudd government also greatly expanded the Howard government's Renewable Energy Target. Despite strenuous efforts by Abbott to scrap it, the RET accounted for more than half of Australia's greenhouse gas abatement between 2011 and 2021.

In health policy, the Gillard government led the world in requiring "plain packaging" (more precisely, packaging with repulsive images of the harms of smoking) for cigarettes. This achievement required a long fight with the forces of Big Tobacco and contributed more broadly to the end of investor–state dispute settlement clauses in trade agreements.

Following the disastrous privatisation of Telstra by the Howard government, Rudd restored public ownership of the telecommunications network through the establishment of the National Broadband Network. Again, despite costly mismanagement under Turnbull, the NBN has been rolled out across the country and is now firmly established.

Finally, by contrast with Albanese's embrace of neoliberal orthodoxy on the economy, the Rudd government embarked on a bold and successful policy of stimulus in response to the global financial crisis. This contrasted sharply with the disastrous austerity policies adopted elsewhere in the world.

This record of achievement can be set against the three main measures Albanese took to the 2022 election: the Voice, the National Anti-Corruption Commission and the Housing Australia Future Fund. The Voice was a disastrous failure, the NACC has been a rolling fiasco and the HAFF was passed only after it was radically remodelled by the Greens.

The Rudd–Gillard government looks limited when its achievements are compared to those of Labor governments in the twentieth century. But it did much more than any other government this century.

John Quiggin

MINORITY REPORT

Response to Correspondence

George Megalogenis

The three months between the publication of my essay and the correspondence contained in this edition have been relatively kind to the major parties. The local economy remains on course for a historic soft landing for Labor, while the political cycle continues to favour the Coalition. The Greens, for their part, may have reached the limits of their parliamentary growth after losing seats at both the ACT and Queensland elections. The three seats the Greens took from the LNP and Labor in Brisbane at the last federal election could easily return to the duopoly based on the state result.

Does that challenge my central thesis about the decline of the two-party system? I am happy to defer to Bill Kelty on the short-term question. As he writes, if Anthony Albanese's government is returned "with a similar or greater margin," then the essay "will be quietly forgotten." A minority Labor government, on the other hand, would vindicate it, while a minority or majority Coalition government would mean the essay "may have got the symptoms right but the cure wrong." While I eschewed predictions in the essay, I cannot see a plausible scenario for an increased majority for Labor. That may change if there is a collapse in support for the Coalition in the one state where it still holds a majority of seats: Queensland. But I doubt that the new LNP premier, David Crisafulli, will gift Albanese the sweetest victory of all. He won't repeat the rookie error of his predecessor, Campbell Newman, by introducing a slash-and-burn budget, at least not before the federal election. Curiously, the LNP's most marginal federal electorate in Queensland is Dutton's own Dickson, on Brisbane's northern fringe. A swing of 1.7 per cent would deliver it to Labor. The next most marginal is Leichhardt, in northern Queensland, where the popular sitting member, Warren Entsch, is retiring. Albanese did tell me that Dickson was on Labor's hit list.

State factors will cut both ways. Albanese will be bracing for a backlash against Jacinta Allan's tired Labor government in Victoria but could offset some losses in traditionally volatile Tasmania, where the Liberal premier, Jeremy Rockliff, leads a divided minority government reliant on the support of the Jacqui Lambie Network. New South Wales and South Australia have popular first-term Labor governments, while Western Australia, the state that helped secure Albanese his majority at the last election, will go to the polls before the federal election is held.

If we zoom back out to consider the changes over the summer, a case can be made for either side winning the secondary contest that will decide who forms a minority government.

Labor should be cheered by the cost-of-living data for the December quarter, which saw the annual inflation rate return to the Reserve Bank's target range of between 2 and 3 per cent. The unemployment rate for December remained steady at 4 per cent. For those policy nerds keeping score, the last time Australia enjoyed an equivalent combination of falling inflation and near-full employment was in the late 1960s. The Prime Minister's Plan A – a dash to the polls after an interest-rate cut – was a live option at the time of writing this reply.

Meanwhile, Peter Dutton's Plan A – to surf the global wave of anti-incumbency to the Lodge – received a boost from the return of Donald Trump to the White House. The US presidential election was held a matter of days after my essay went to the printer, so there was no point in me speculating on the result or its implications for Australian politics. But I can do so now because Dutton seems to be carrying Trump's executive orders in his jacket pocket as a form of political thesaurus, from which he lifts attack lines for his own culture war.

His appointment of Jacinta Nampijinpa Price to the shadow portfolio for government efficiency was a direct copy of Trump's Department of Government Efficiency, headed by the world's richest man, Elon Musk. Dutton may be leading with his chin on this one because a key plank of Labor's re-election campaign is the fear card of Coalition spending cuts. Dutton still carries the baggage of the 2014 budget. He was the health minister responsible for its most politically damaging measure: the $7 co-payment for visits to the GP and for out-of-hospital imaging and pathology services. Albanese had underlined this very point in our interview last August. Part of Labor's response to the inflation shock, he said, "is about strengthening Medicare, which is a particular weakness of Mr Dutton's as he was the health minister who tried to wreck Medicare."

Dutton followed Price's appointment with an appearance on the ABC's *Insiders* program in which he said the Coalition would cut spending but would wait till after the election to decide what items in the budget it would target. Any reasonably competent government should be able to translate that sloppy answer into a reason for voters to stick with the devil they know. If there is a surprise result in

Labor's favour, whether a narrow majority or a comfortable minority with a clear lead over the Coalition on the floor of the parliament, it will be because it nailed Mediscare Mark II.

Trump governs against the very idea of government. I liken his approach to the Bush administration's scorched-earth occupation of Iraq, where the bureaucracy was decapitated along with Saddam Hussein's regime. Watch this space, because Trump's campaign to liberate Americans from what he calls the "deep state" and the "swamp" will create a dilemma for Dutton. Does the Opposition leader really want to be associated with the chaos that will inevitably follow as frontline services are compromised by the president's war on woke?

Where Dutton can draw comfort from Trump's example is that the politics of punching-down on minorities works best in a cost-of-living crisis. What I can't tell with the election still two or three months away is whether Dutton's strongman campaign will tempt New Australians in the outer suburbs to shift from Labor to Liberal in sufficient numbers to topple the Albanese government.

*

I am grateful to every correspondent who took time out of their summer holidays to read the essay and write a response for these pages.

Bill Kelty has written the definitive account of where the wealth created since the global financial crisis has gone. It's a soberingly long list of politically privileged Australians and just one outsider group: "property owners, shareholders, the very rich, executives, retirees and some recipients of the NDIS (National Disability Insurance Scheme)."

Labor has governed for seven of the fifteen years he covers in his analysis, and he is right to divide the blame equally between his side of politics and the Coalition. As he notes, "The Albanese government may be the first Labor government since James Scullin's that has not left working people better off at the end of its term than they were at the start."

Judith Brett and Sam Roggeveen highlight a factor I left out of the essay that helps explains the decline of the major parties: the hollowing out of their respective membership bases. Sam is kind enough to acknowledge that this angle was beyond the scope of the essay. Nonetheless, I was wrong not to mention it.

Judith's insight that "debate, negotiation and consensus-building is shifting from inside the parties back to the parliament, where they were for most of the nineteenth and early twentieth centuries," is spot on.

Ben Raue raises an interesting question about the limitations of single-member electorates as the votes of the major parties decline. He writes: "In the future, we could see parties winning large seat numbers off relatively low votes, and a worsening relationship between how people vote and who is elected." I would add that the most recent British election is a window into that future, albeit in a parliament in which seats are decided on a first-past-the-post basis rather than our compulsory preferential system. British Labour won two-thirds of the seats in the House of Commons with just one-third of the primary vote.

I found Ben's explanation of the structural reasons for the Labor–Greens rivalry persuasive and agree that the relatively high Labor vote in teal electorates means that any support the teals give to a minority Albanese government would be less controversial than the decision of Tony Windsor and Rob Oakeshott to back Julia Gillard over Tony Abbott in 2010.

Thank you, Peter Lewis, for sharing some of your research. The line that jumped off the page for me was the electorate's "contradictory desire for government to intervene more assertively along with a simultaneous lack of faith that such intervention will make any material difference."

I've reflected on John Quiggin's expansive list of Labor's achievements in office under the Rudd and Gillard governments and agree that I should have added the National Broadband Network and the Renewable Energy Target to my much shorter summary. However, I think the jury is still out on the Renewable Energy Target. Dutton may yet unpick it in office.

Finally, to the bait laid by my friend and colleague at the old Melbourne *Sun News-Pictorial* Joel Deane. The role of our former employer, News Limited, was off-topic for the essay, but I am happy to tease out the argument Joel raises about the consequences of Labor's cross-media reforms in the 1980s, which handed The Herald and Weekly Times to Rupert Murdoch. That deal transformed News, then a minnow in the Australian market, into the dominant player in our print media. I encourage researchers to take up Joel's challenge to check whether most working journalists today have drawn a salary from Murdoch at one point in their career. But I wonder if that would settle the matter.

I think the dumbing-down of the Australian media is a more complex story. The hollowing-out of the ABC – an active policy choice made by both Labor and Coalition governments over the past decade and a half – is an equal if not greater factor than what Joel describes as the "blokey, knee-jerk, punitive culture" at News. The irony is that the very best journalists at the ABC are former colleagues of mine at *The Australian*, Laura Tingle and Alan Kohler.

I have always been a sceptic of the role of News in influencing elections. Many colleagues – although not Joel – are prone to the easy conspiracy theory that Rupert decides who runs this country. Let's start with the three states where Murdoch acquired the biggest-selling newspapers as part of the HWT takeover – Victoria, Queensland and South Australia. Labor won seven of the past ten state elections in Victoria on Murdoch's watch; eleven out of thirteen in Queensland; and six of nine in South Australia. Readers of the *Herald Sun*, in particular, would be perplexed that "Dictator Dan" Andrews secured back-to-back landslides in Victoria on either side of the pandemic, in 2018 and then 2022. The strongest Coalition state in the Murdoch era happened to be the one he didn't keep from the HWT, Western Australia, where the Coalition won four of the nine elections held in that time.

The federal cycle does lean slightly to the Coalition. But if the Albanese government is returned, in whatever form, Labor and the Coalition will have won seven elections each since Rupert marched into the Flinders Street headquarters of the HWT in 1987.

Remember that Rupert was still on Team Keating well into the second term of the Howard government, as evidenced by the support that all his newspapers gave to the republic referendum in 1999. In fact, he remained a true believer for longer than the Labor Party itself, which, as Bill Kelty reminds us, "walked away from Hawke and Keating after the 1996 election."

What is certainly true is that News Limited has affected the tone of political debate in Australia since it threw its uncritical support behind Abbott in 2010. It remains to be seen whether its uncritical support for Dutton will end in the same category of regret, with a government that self-sabotaged because it didn't feel the need to take policy seriously.

George Megalogenis

Judith Brett is emeritus professor of politics at La Trobe University. A former editor of *Meanjin* and columnist for *The Age*, she won the National Biography Award in 2018 for *The Enigmatic Mr Deakin*. She is the author of four Quarterly Essays.

Joel Deane is a poet, novelist and speechwriter.

Jess Hill is an investigative journalist, the author of *See What You Made Me Do* and *The Reckoning*, and one of Australia's most recognised and respected thinkers on gendered violence. In addition to her broadcast work – two highly acclaimed docu-series on SBS and a podcast titled *The Trap* – she has spoken at almost 400 events across the country. Her work has won three Walkley Awards, an Amnesty International Award and the Stella Prize in 2020. In 2023, she was named *Marie Claire* Changemaker of the Year and in 2024, the NSW Premier's Woman of Excellence.

Bill Kelty is a former secretary of the Australian Council of Trade Unions (1983 to 2000).

Peter Lewis is executive director of progressive research and communications firm Essential. He is a regular columnist for *Guardian Australia* and the founder of Per Capita's Centre of the Public Square. He is the author of five books, including *Webtopia* and *The Public Square Project*.

George Megalogenis is the author of four Quarterly Essays. His book *The Australian Moment* won the 2013 Prime Minister's Literary Award for Non-fiction and the 2012 Walkley Award for Non-fiction. He is also the author of *Faultlines*, *The Longest Decade*, *Australia's Second Chance* and *The Football Solution*.

John Quiggin is an Australian Laureate Fellow in economics at the University of Queensland and the author of *Zombie Economics* and *Economics in Two Lessons*. His blog, at johnquiggin.com, presents commentary from a social-democratic viewpoint.

Ben Raue is an independent electoral analyst and the creator of *The Tally Room* website and podcast. He has provided election night commentary for ABC Radio and *Guardian Australia* and published several book chapters analysing Australian election results.

Sam Roggeveen is director of the International Security Program at the Lowy Institute and author of *Our Very Own Brexit* and *The Echidna Strategy*.

QUARTERLY ESSAY BACK ISSUES

- ☐ **QE 1** *In Denial* by Robert Manne $27.99
- ☐ **QE 2** *Appeasing Jakarta* by John Birmingham $27.99
- ☐ **QE 3** *The Opportunist* by Guy Rundle $27.99
- ☐ **QE 4** *Rabbit Syndrome* by Don Watson $27.99
- ☐ **QE 5** *Girt By Sea* by Mungo MacCallum $27.99
- ☐ **QE 6** *Beyond Belief* by John Button $27.99
- ☐ **QE 7** *Paradise Betrayed* by John Martinkus $27.99
- **QE 8** *Groundswell* by Amanda Lohrey OUT OF STOCK
- ☐ **QE 9** *Beautiful Lies* by Tim Flannery $27.99
- ☐ **QE 10** *Bad Company* by Gideon Haigh $27.99
- ☐ **QE 11** *Whitefella Jump Up* by Germaine Greer $27.99
- ☐ **QE 12** *Made in England* by David Malouf $27.99
- ☐ **QE 13** *Sending Them Home* by Robert Manne with David Corlett $27.99
- ☐ **QE 14** *Mission Impossible* by Paul McGeough $27.99
- ☐ **QE 15** *Latham's World* by Margaret Simons $27.99
- ☐ **QE 16** *Breach of Trust* by Raimond Gaita $27.99
- ☐ **QE 17** *'Kangaroo Court'* by John Hirst $27.99
- ☐ **QE 18** *The Worried Well* by Gail Bell $27.99
- ☐ **QE 19** *Relaxed & Comfortable* by Judith Brett $27.99
- ☐ **QE 20** *A Time for War* by John Birmingham $27.99
- ☐ **QE 21** *What's Left? by Clive Hamilton* $27.99
- ☐ **QE 22** *Voting for Jesus* by Amanda Lohrey $27.99
- ☐ **QE 23** *The History Question* by Inga Clendinnen $27.99
- ☐ **QE 24** *No Fixed Address* by Robyn Davidson $27.99
- ☐ **QE 25** *Bipolar Nation* by Peter Hartcher $27.99
- ☐ **QE 26** *His Master's Voice* by David Marr $27.99
- ☐ **QE 27** *Reaction Time* by Ian Lowe $27.99
- ☐ **QE 28** *Exit Right* by Judith Brett $27.99
- ☐ **QE 29** *Love & Money* by Anne Manne $27.99
- ☐ **QE 30** *Last Drinks* by Paul Toohey $27.99
- ☐ **QE 31** *Now or Never* by Tim Flannery $27.99
- ☐ **QE 32** *American Revolution* by Kate Jennings $27.99
- ☐ **QE 33** *Quarry Vision* by Guy Pearse $27.99
- ☐ **QE 34** *Stop at Nothing* by Annabel Crabb $27.99
- ☐ **QE 35** *Radical Hope* by Noel Pearson $27.99
- ☐ **QE 36** *Australian Story* by Mungo MacCallum $27.99
- ☐ **QE 37** *What's Right?* by Waleed Aly $27.99
- ☐ **QE 38** *Power Trip* by David Marr $27.99
- ☐ **QE 39** *Power Shift* by Hugh White $27.99
- ☐ **QE 40** *Trivial Pursuit* by George Megalogenis $27.99
- ☐ **QE 41** *The Happy Life* by David Malouf $27.99
- ☐ **QE 42** *Fair Share* by Judith Brett $27.99
- ☐ **QE 43** *Bad News* by Robert Manne $27.99
- ☐ **QE 44** *Man-Made World* by Andrew Charlton $27.99
- ☐ **QE 45** *Us and Them* by Anna Krien $27.99
- ☐ **QE 46** *Great Expectations* by Laura Tingle $27.99
- ☐ **QE 47** *Political Animal* by David Marr $27.99
- ☐ **QE 48** *After the Future* by Tim Flannery $27.99
- ☐ **QE 49** *Not Dead Yet* by Mark Latham $27.99
- ☐ **QE 50** *Unfinished Business* by Anna Goldsworthy $27.99
- ☐ **QE 51** *The Prince* by David Marr $27.99
- ☐ **QE 52** *Found in Translation* by Linda Jaivin $27.99
- ☐ **QE 53** *That Sinking Feeling* by Paul Toohey $27.99
- ☐ **QE 54** *Dragon's Tail* by Andrew Charlton $27.99
- ☐ **QE 55** *A Rightful Place* by Noel Pearson $27.99
- ☐ **QE 56** *Clivosaurus* by Guy Rundle $27.99
- ☐ **QE 57** *Dear Life* by Karen Hitchcock $27.99
- ☐ **QE 58** *Blood Year* by David Kilcullen $27.99
- ☐ **QE 59** *Faction Man* by David Marr $27.99
- ☐ **QE 60** *Political Amnesia* by Laura Tingle $27.99
- ☐ **QE 61** *Balancing Act* by George Megalogenis $27.99
- ☐ **QE 62** *Firing Line* by James Brown $27.99
- ☐ **QE 63** *Enemy Within* by Don Watson $27.99
- ☐ **QE 64** *The Australian Dream* by Stan Grant $27.99
- ☐ **QE 65** *The White Queen* by David Marr $27.99
- ☐ **QE 66** *The Long Goodbye* by Anna Krien $27.99
- ☐ **QE 67** *Moral Panic 101* by Benjamin Law $27.99
- ☐ **QE 68** *Without America* by Hugh White $27.99

QUARTERLY ESSAY BACK ISSUES

- ☐ **QE 69** *Moment of Truth* by Mark McKenna $27.99
- ☐ **QE 70** *Dead Right* by Richard Denniss $27.99
- ☐ **QE 71** *Follow the Leader* by Laura Tingle $27.99
- ☐ **QE 72** *Net Loss* by Sebastian Smee $27.99
- ☐ **QE 73** *Australia Fair* by Rebecca Huntley $27.99
- ☐ **QE 74** *The Prosperity Gospel* by Erik Jensen $27.99
- ☐ **QE 75** *Men at Work* by Annabel Crabb $27.99
- ☐ **QE 76** *Red Flag* by Peter Hartcher $27.99
- ☐ **QE 77** *Cry Me a River* by Margaret Simons $27.99
- ☐ **QE 78** *The Coal Curse* by Judith Brett $27.99
- ☐ **QE 79** *The End of Certainty* by Katharine Murphy $27.99
- ☐ **QE 80** *The High Road* by Laura Tingle $27.99
- ☐ **QE 81** *Getting to Zero* by Alan Finkel $27.99
- ☐ **QE 82** *Exit Strategy* by George Megalogenis $27.99
- ☐ **QE 83** *Top Blokes* by Lech Blaine $27.99
- ☐ **QE 84** *The Reckoning* by Jess Hill $27.99
- ☐ **QE 85** *Not Waving, Drowning* by Sarah Krasnostein $27.99
- ☐ **QE 86** *Sleepwalk to War* by Hugh White $27.99
- ☐ **QE 87** *Uncivil Wars* by Waleed Aly & Scott Stephens $27.99
- ☐ **QE 88** *Lone Wolf* by Katharine Murphy $27.99
- ☐ **QE 89** *The Wires That Bind* by Saul Griffith $27.99
- ☐ **QE 90** *Voice of Reason* by Megan Davis $27.99
- ☐ **QE 91** *Lifeboat* by Micheline Lee $27.99
- ☐ **QE 92** *The Great Divide* by Alan Kohler $27.99
- ☐ **QE 93** *Bad Cop* by Lech Blaine $27.99
- ☐ **QE 94** *Highway to Hell* by Joëlle Gergis $27.99
- ☐ **QE 95** *High Noon* by Don Watson $27.99
- ☐ **QE 96** *Minority Report* by George Megalogenis $29.99

Order back issues online

Prices include GST.
$10 flat-rate shipping within Australia.
Please include this form with delivery and payment details overleaf.
Back issues also available as ebooks from ebook retailers.